A PHILOSOPHICALL DISCOURSE
CONCERNING SPEECH
(1668)
AND
A DISCOURSE WRITTEN TO
A LEARNED FRIER
(1670)

HISTORY OF PSYCHOLOGY SERIES

GENERAL INTRODUCTION

The historically interesting works reprinted in this series helped to prepare the way for the science of psychology. Most of these books are long forgotten, but their relevance to the field is unmistakable. Many of the writings on mental and moral philosophy, published before the dawn of scientific procedures, have much to commend them to present-day scholars. These books serve as groundwork for a fuller account of the background from which the field emerged, and they should be attractive to students who seek in the past for hints of the future direction that certain types of research can take. Each work will have an Introduction stating the provenance and significance of the book and will add appropriate biographical information.

ROBERT I. WATSON
General Editor

University of New Hampshire

A PHILOSOPHICALL DISCOURSE CONCERNING SPEECH

(1668)

AND

A DISCOURSE WRITTEN TO A LEARNED FRIER

(1670)

GÉRAUD DE CORDEMOY

FACSIMILE REPRODUCTIONS
WITH AN INTRODUCTION
BY BARBARA ROSS

SCHOLARS' FACSIMILES & REPRINTS
DELMAR, NEW YORK
1972

A Philosophicall Discourse Concerning Speech
A Discourse Written to a Learned Frier

Facsimile re-editions published by
Scholars' Facsimiles & Reprints, Inc.,
Post Office Box 344, Delmar, New York 12054

Reproduced from copies in
and with permission of
The Houghton Library, Harvard University

Printed in the United States of America

Library of Congress Cataloging in Publication Data

Cordemoy, Géraud de, d. 1684.
    A philosophicall discourse concerning speech (1668) and A discourse
written to a learned frier (1670).

    (History of psychology series)
    Translation of the author's Discours physique de la parole and his
Copie d'une lettre écrite à un sçavent religieux de la Compagnie de Jésus.
    Includes bibliographical references.
    1. Languages—Philosophy. I. Cordemoy, Géraud de, d. 1684. Copie
d'une lettre écrite à un sçavent religieux de la Compagnie de Jésus.
English. 1972. II. Title. III. Title: A discourse written to a learned frier.
P101.C7313   1668a   401   72-6400
ISBN 0-8201-1106-6

INTRODUCTION*

THE TWO seventeenth-century works of Géraud de Cordemoy (1626–1684)[1] included in this volume illustrate some of the major concerns of scientists, philosophers, and theologians during a period which witnessed the culmination of two concurrent revolutions: a drastic change in the framework within which man viewed himself and his universe, and a general acceptance of a new approach to the study of the natural sciences.

Until the seventeenth century, the intellectual structure for man's perceptions about himself and the phenomena of nature were provided, for the most part, by ancient philosophy; and, since the Middle Ages, Scholasticism, which had set up Aristotle and the Scriptures as its authority, prescribed the boundaries within which explanations were to be kept. During the seventeenth century, however, Scholasticism came under strong attack. Developments accruing over several hundred years contributed to the change. The widening of geographical boundaries and improved methods of communication revealed evidence contrary to traditional sources; and, as observation after observation uncovered insuperable contradictions with the epical scheme, alternative solutions were attempted. Man's place in nature became a topic of serious debate.

In 1664, Henry Power (1623–1669) wrote in his now classic *Experimental Philosophy:*

> This is the Age wherein (methinks) Philosophy comes in with a Spring-tide; and the Peripateticks may as well hope to stop the Current of the Tide, or (with *Xerxes*) to fetter the Ocean, as hinder the overflowing of free Philosophy: Methinks, I see how all the old Rubbish must be thrown away, and the rotten Buildings be overthrown, and carried away with so powerful an Inundation.[2]

Change, albeit inevitable, happens neither suddenly nor silently. To understand Cordemoy's contribution, we must examine some aspects of what has been called the "scientific revolution."

What had been generally accepted as "truth" or "explanation" came into question in the seventeenth century. It became evident to some, particularly those who promoted and practiced the "new philosophy" of

---

* I am indebted to Dr. Otto Marx for his helpful comments on an earlier draft of this Introduction.

Francis Bacon (1561–1626), that reliance on the classics as traditionally done lent little or nothing to new ideas in the natural sciences; and, more important, traditional explanations proved to be inadequate, and often inaccurate. Various philosophies which ran counter to traditionalism were promoted, and the ensuing conflict involved a constant dialogue between those who held to traditional beliefs and those who sought new solutions for the phenomena of nature.

Those who opposed scholasticism and proposed new methods of inquiry with which to understand nature did not mean to dispel religious beliefs, but wanted to rid the natural sciences of the traditional, vitalistic interpretations. Theological subject matter and scientific questions, they proposed, should be treated in different contexts and each studied by different methods. However, metaphysical, theological, and scientific questions were so intertwined that any attempts at a reconciliation between science and religion proved controversial. Related issues and consequences exerted decisive influence upon all subsequent history, including the field of psychology.

Two major developments of particular importance in the history of psychology confronted seventeenth-century philosophers and scientists, as a drastic change in the conception of the relations between soul and body came about. William Harvey (1578–1657) offered a mechanical explanation for the circulation of the blood in 1628,[3] and by so doing, removed the Aristotelian "vital forces" from the arteries and veins. This was a blow to the Scholastics. A second setback to the Aristotelian tradition was Descartes' (1596–1650) proposal that animal body was purely material, and all animal actions purely mechanical. By including animals in his mechanistic universe, Descartes subjected them to physical laws. Moreover, Descartes included man's body as subject matter which could be understood through methods of natural science. He wrote, ". . . the greater part of our motions do not depend on the mind at all . . . ."[4]

In the Middle Ages man had been set apart from natural laws because he had a soul, and was subject only to his own willfulness and that of God. Not only the soul, but the body of man was sacrosanct. Descartes' conception of the body of man as mechanical, which relegated free will to the immaterial soul, freed the body of man for objective examination. The revival of Greek medicine also contributed to this trend. For Descartes, since animals had no soul, they too, were accessible for experimentation. By placing lower animal and man into the same conceptual framework as natural phenomena, Descartes shifted the attention from soul to body. The transition was not complete, however, merely upon the expression of Descartes' views.

Strong reactions to Descartes' physics and metaphysics led to voluminous polemical writings surrounding the traditional, vitalistic explanation of bodily movements which embodied an indwelling immaterial force, and Descartes' mechanistic explanation. The vitalist-mechanist issue was, perhaps, the most urgent matter in the seventeenth century.

Several aspects of Descartes' philosophy were left in an unsatisfactory state thereby compounding the controversy surrounding his system. Descartes' disciples were left to elucidate, modify, or extend his mechanical views. In need of refinement were three interrelated issues: Descartes' definition of matter; reliance on human speech as the basis for the man-brute distinction; and, the problem of the mind-body relationship. Géraud de Cordemoy made major contributions to the solutions of all three. It is to those contributions and the historical context in which they were produced that we now turn.

A clear understanding of the distinction between mind and matter was preliminary to the comprehension of Cartesian physics, according to Cordemoy. He took Descartes' treatment of matter as his focal point in *Six Discours sur la distinction et l'union du corps et de l'âme.* The work, never translated into English but available in Latin, was published in 1666,[5] and is better known as *Discernement du corps et de l'âme.* It was a strong statement about Cartesian dualism and its relationship to physical science. Cordemoy expands on that statement in the first book reprinted in the present volume. *A philosophicall Discourse concerning Speech, conformable to the Cartesian Principles . . .* (1668).[6] For the most part both writings were in support of Descartes' physics; however, Cordemoy saw some need for modification and clarification if the mechanical system was to be accepted more widely. Cordemoy proposed that Descartes' definition of matter as one extended substance failed to explain movement and rest, and left no room for distinguishing one thing from another. That is, the reduction of all substances to one tends to obliterate differences among things. There were many other Cartesians who shared Cordemoy's opinion,[7] which was a preference for the use of the term "matter" as a collective or general expression of an assemblage of bodies or atoms. Cordemoy defined units of composition as extended substance, and each unit as indivisible.

Not all Cartesians accepted Cordemoy's atomistic development of

Descartes' theory of matter. An intimate friend of Cordemoy's wrote to a M. de Gaumont:

> il est vrai, comme j'ai reconnu depuis, que M. Cordemoy abandonnait Descartes sur plusieirs points, sur le monde indéfini, sur l'impossibilité du vide, sur la divisibilité de la matière à l'infin, et sur l'essence de la matière qu'il ne mettait pas dans l'etendue.[8]

Cordemoy was accused of weakening Descartes' position and strengthening that of Gassendi, who subscribed to the atomistic and empirical doctrines.[9] Pierre Gassendi (1592–1655) has been presented as a precursor to Descartes, who is said to have considered Gassendi an authority in scientific matters.[10] Originally, some degree of reason was attributed to animals by Gassendi, but he later implied that animals had a material soul. Descartes' earlier admiration for Gassendi appears to have dissipated after reading his objections to "Meditations".[11] But, for present purposes, the relationship between Cordemoy and Gassendi is pertinent. The two men agreed on the notion of animal automatism; they differed, however, in their account of man's superiority. Possession of a soul made man different in kind from the standpoint of Cordemoy, who strongly supported Cartesian dualism; Gassendi's philosophy of Epicurean atomism, which postulated matter as the sole reality led him to attribute man's superiority to superior corporeal organization;[12] thus, man was different from animals or brutes only in degree. Despite some criticism of Cordemoy's modifications of Descartes' treatment of matter,[13] most of Cordemoy's contemporaries considered him a *grand cartésien*.

The demonstration of human speech as distinctly different from animal communication was the crucial test, one might say, in demonstrating the existence of soul in man and the lack of soul in animals. Descartes argued that if brutes possessed intelligence or reason or had thoughts, that since they had the necessary physiological equipment with which to express them, they could indeed do so.[14] However, he did not develop his argument fully. Cordemoy does so in the first work in the present volume, *A philosophicall Discourse concerning Speech, conformable to the Cartesian Principles* . . . (1668). He examined the relationship between structure and function of bodily organs related to speech and concluded that beasts communicate, but only in a mechanical way, and that although animals are able to distinguish objects through sense impressions, they do not have the ability to form compound ideas or abstractions. He suggests that the behavior of animals is habitual and related to more immediate stimuli than humans, who detach themselves from the concrete and operate at an abstract level. Only those who "can agree that what signifies one thing can also signify another" have bodies united to souls and enjoy intelligence or reason. Man's ability to abstract and to give signs of one's thoughts indicate that he has perception which resides in the soul.[15] Thought cannot be identified simply with the use of language however, as words are only one aspect of the thought process.

Cordemoy's analysis of thinking is remarkably similar to one of the most popular definitions of recent years, John Dewey's characterization of thought as problem-solving behavior. Dewey's conception emphasized the development of thought as a means to enable men to adapt to a difficult and hostile environment. Once the environment has been brought under control, thought becomes more automatic and spontaneous. Cordemoy's analysis is similar, but he finds instances in man which go beyond basic self-preservation.

Language and thought interact in the course of a person's development, according to Cordemoy. The development of speech in children is progressive from the concrete to the abstract,[16] and the elements of grammar are an imitation of precepts "which Nature gives to Children." He proposes that children pay attention to certain signs and learn particular words in order to fulfill their needs. Furthermore, without being taught, children learn many things "by the sole force of their attention."

Cordemoy presents instances which demonstrate that man's thought process is not always utilitarian only at the very practical, adaptive level. The possession of a soul is for a higher purpose—it is the means through which man comes to understand nature and God.

Cordemoy not only presents a theory of speech and thought but also furthers Descartes' statements regarding sensation as adaptive, and distinguishes more clearly than had Descartes, the neurological process of sensation from perception (the thought process itself); and man from brute.

The proposal that animal body was purely material, and that all animal actions were purely mechanical was a natural extension of Descartes' insistence on the separation of matter and mind, or the material and immaterial. Although animal automatism gradually came to be acceptable to more philosophers during the 1670s, there were still considerations of a theological nature which fostered an ambivalence for many who could not reconcile religious and scientific views, or who had differences of opinion regarding God's role. The revival of materialism such as that reflected in Descartes gave occasion to numerous attempts to establish the spiritual nature of reality, as the man-brute distinction became the basis for controversy.

The first major controversy was between the Cartesians and the Traditionalists. The latter's position was that brutes possessed an animal soul, which was intermediate between matter and spirit; it allowed feeling, imagination, and memory. The Peripatetics were formidable opponents of Cartesianism for several reasons: the traditional view of a hierarchy created by God was destroyed by Descartes' man-brute distinction; and, Descartes' method of investigation refused reliance on any previous authority, thereby discrediting Scholasticism. Most Scholastic arguments against the man-brute distinction were on religious grounds with the aim of discrediting Cartesianism as a whole. Yet, rejection of animal mechanism did not necessarily indicate rejection of all aspects of Cartesianism; likewise, acceptance of animal automatism did not indicate acceptance of Cartesian philosophy as a whole.[17] Consequently, polemics varied.

Descartes' concept of soul was spiritual, incorporeal, immortal; if animal soul as proposed by the Scholastics was a spiritual substance, it was immaterial, and thus, immortal. Neither the Scholastics nor the Cartesians could accept such a notion. Or, one could argue that the human soul was not immortal, but was a spiritual substance; spirituality and immateriality would not, then, imply immortality. This was not acceptable either, since the mechanical philosophy as well as that of the traditionalists negated such a possibility. If animals were accepted as entirely mechanistic as suggested by Descartes and argued by Cordemoy, there was the possible danger to the traditionalists that the mechanical nature of man's bodily processes might be extended to include the mind or soul as well. Traditional religious views appeared threatened, despite the fact that Descartes never disavowed God's intended superiority of man which was retained in the concept of a thinking immaterial soul.

Descartes was accused of atheism by a Jesuit and devoted Aristotelian, Gabriel Cossart (1615–1674), who was a professor of humanities at Clermont College from 1642–1656. Cordemoy answers Cossart's accusations in *A Discourse written to a learned frier . . .*,[18] which is the second work included in the present volume. Cordemoy believed in the immortality of man's soul as had Descartes, and in his letter to Cossart, he defends animal mechanism by turning to the Scriptures. Descartes' writings and the Bible are compared on critical points, and Cordemoy concludes that Descartes' principles are a more extended and exact way of explaining what was already said in the Scriptures. Despite minor differences between Descartes and the Bible, Cordemoy argues that if what Descartes said is dangerous, then the Bible is also dangerous. Cordemoy's reply to Cossart stirred up the important issue of Descartes' religious views, which was of particular concern to the Jesuits and other traditionalists.

Gaston Pardies (1636–1673), a Jesuit and a confrere of Cordemoy's at l'Academie Bourdelot, promoted the traditional position in *Discours de la Conoissance des Bestes*, first published in 1672.[19] Indicative of the interest in the subject, by 1724 seven editions including Latin and Italian translations had appeared. Pardies provided support for the view that beasts, though they lacked intellectual knowledge, had sensible knowledge; they differed from man only in degree.

Related to the man-brute controversy was Descartes' reliance on the pineal gland[20] as the organ of interaction between the body and soul in man. Descartes wrote:

> . . . the machine of the body is so formed that from the simple fact that this gland is diversely moved by the soul, or by such other cause, whatever it is, it thrusts the spirits which surround it towards the pores of the brain, which conduct them by the nerves into the muscles, by which means it causes them to move the limbs.[21]

A major threat to Cartesian dualism occurred when a contemporary of Cordemoy's, Nicholas Steno (1638–1686),[22] exposed Descartes' error concerning the pineal gland as a point of interaction between mind and body in *Discourse on the Anatomy of the Brain* presented during the early part of 1666.[23] Pierre Huet, a friend of Cordemoy, received a letter referring to Steno's experiment:

> . . . Stenson, the Dane, has performed the most marvelous experiments ever in this field. He has even forced the obstinate and dogmatic Cartesians to admit the error of their leader with regard to the gland of the brain and its function . . . .[24]

In the 3 June 1667 issue of the *Philosophical Transactions of the Royal Society of London* is reference to a letter from Italy, written by Steno describing one of his experiments which discredited Descartes' proposals regarding the mind-body relationship:

> . . . A Tortoise had its head cut off, and yet was found to move its foot three days after. Here was no Communication with the *Conarium*.[25] As this seems to have given a sore blow to the *Car-*

tesian Doctrine, so the Disciples thereof are here endeavoring to heal the wound.[26]

Steno approved of Descartes' mechanism, but for obvious reasons rejected his anatomical descriptions.[27]

Cartesian physiologists elaborated on the theory of automatism by explaining the functioning of the sensory system in man in mechanical terms. In the 17th century, physiologists and anatomists, following the empirical method, examined movement and consciousness in relation to the brain primarily as a physiological problem. They granted that behavior of a voluntary nature might involve both body and soul, but that involuntary responses were to be studied and explained without recourse to the soul.

A firm mechanist who worked out a theory of neuro-muscular activity along purely mechanical lines was Giovanni A. Borelli (1608–1679), who frequented l'Academie Bourdelot in the company of Cordemoy, Pardies, and Steno. In *De Motu Animalium* (1680–81),[28] which was published posthumously, Borelli advanced Steno's work on muscular motion. Borelli rejected incorporeal and aereal substances as activators of a muscle; he dealt with musclar action from the vantage point of a mathematician and mechanist, and offered a more materialistic explanation than had Descartes.[29]

The physiological doctrine of the body-machine elaborated by iatro-mechanists such as Steno and Borelli was generally accepted by the end of the seventeenth century, as increasing scepticism of traditional accounts stressed the pertinence of the issue to natural science rather than to theology.[30]

Certainly, the intention of seventeenth-century physiologists was not to examine the rational or immaterial soul of man within the same context as bodily actions; they simply believed that the workings of the human body could be understood best in mechanical terms. But, as studies on the central nervous system continued and evidence accumulated, the implications were often what neither the ancients nor the moderns wanted to see. Unpredictable results caused serious difficulties which had to be explained. But, one must ask what sorts of explanations were admissible at all? Certainly not that man possessed no immaterial or spiritual soul. But the problem of the mind-body relationship continued to plague Cartesians.

Cordemoy offered a solution. He rejected interactionism, Descartes' proposal that a sensation received into the mind could create movement, and also the notion that the rational soul could direct connections between sensory input and motor response.[31] These were all weaknesses in Descartes' philosophy which were under attack. Cordemoy explained the mind-body relationship on the basis of occasionalism.[32] He held that the phenomena of the mind and body are only the occasion for each other, there being no causal connection between them. Man does not move his limbs because he wills to do so; man wills to move them, but God becomes the efficient cause and carries out the design. Thus, mind is but the "occasional cause" and God's constant intervention explains the apparent union between mind and body. The genuine religious feelings regarding the superiority of man and God's role were beyond dispute with Cordemoy's alternative.

A French historian of Cartesian philosophy refers to Cordemoy as the "first" occasionalist;[33] however, Nicolas de Malebranche (1638–1715), Cordemoy's contemporary, is perhaps best known among the early promoters of occasionalism. Malebranche, like Cordemoy, promoted animal automatism. In his early writing Malebranche appeared to support Cordemoy's position on the indivisibility of matter; later, however, Malebranche's position changed. Nevertheless, the two men shared many views, and Malebranche cited Cordemoy often in *Recherche de la Vérité*.[34] Almost a century later, Julien Offray de La Mettrie (1709–1751) expressed admiration for Malebranche's ingenuity in working out the details of a mechanistic psychophysiology, which, if one ignored the dualistic and religious aspects of Malebranche's thinking as did La Mettrie, approached materialism.[35]

The final step was perhaps inevitable. Cartesian dualism became a materialistic monism, and the argument of animal automatism took the more explicit form of man the machine with the publication of La Mettrie's *L'Homme Machine* in 1747. La Mettrie found some aspects of the anti-metaphysical, sensationalist psychology of Locke appealing as an alternative to the Cartesian doctrine of innate ideas. Considerable importance was given by La Mettrie to education and the environment, and the organic similarity between ape and man led him to attempt, unsuccessfully, to instruct an ape to speak. He no doubt felt compelled to find experimental proof for a mechanistic explanation of language to support his man-machine thesis. Recall that Cordemoy and other Cartesians had convincingly argued that the ability to speak was the crucial trait that distinguished man from beast.

Both Cordemoy and La Mettrie treated words or symbols as facilitators of thought, and as only approximate expressions of reality. Thinking, both suggested, was facilitated through the use of language which becomes an ordering of signs in many patterns. La Mettrie, however, implied that the idea in the sensation and understanding were the same; Cordemoy overcame that difficulty in his sharp distinction between the physical and psychological. But then, La Mettrie's assumption of monism created a problem; Cordemoy, a dualist, who brought God into his theory of language and thought, was faced with no contradictions.

A thoroughgoing mechanist, La Mettrie ignored problems related to the nature of the soul and conjectures about God's role in the thought process. He explained the differences between man and animals on the basis of complexity of bodily organization, combined with the educational process.

Prior efforts to clarify metaphysically the nature of mind to the satisfaction of all had failed; La Mettrie was writing in a world of changing circumstances in the 18th century, yet he rightly anticipated that his proposal to restate the problems of mind as a problem of physics would be met with strong protest. He was censored in France,[36] and was forced to leave Holland because of his outspoken materialism.

The continuing controversy of vitalism-mechanism in the eighteenth century was carried on, among others, by Georg Ernst Stahl (1660–1734), a German physician, who supported a vitalistic view of the mind-body relationship. He postulated a substantial but incorporeal moving power as a link between soul and body, and challenged the mechanistic view. The debate wore on.

The task of the historian of psychology, I believe, is to examine past ideas, issues, and problems related to the nature of man within particular intellectual environments. By doing so, he has greater understanding regarding the merits of issues within particular contexts.

Although the mind-body, man-brute, vitalism-mechanism issues are often dismissed as passe by psychologists, controversies bearing on these problems recur frequently in slightly different form. The retention of mechanistic ideas by behaviorally oriented psychologists allow the possibility of psychology as a natural science; and, since science by its very nature, it is assumed, deals with phenomena that are causally determinable, physical or psychical facts which remain basically unpredictable lie outside the realm of science. Behaviorally oriented psychologists do not deny phenomenological variants, but rather, choose to ignore them. To ignore them, however, the phenomenologists argue, is to deny man an essential part of his nature.

From one generation to another, men slide into a world of apparently new issues; yet, underlying much of psychology today, as was true in speculations about the nature of man in the seventeenth century, is the search for a logically consistent and scientifically acceptable account of the relations between subjective immediate experience on the one hand, and behavioral processes on the other.

Balz reminds us:

> If we dismiss the controversy concerning the soul of the brute as unreal we begin to suspect that a similar judgment concerning issues of today would be equally justified. The more we linger over the details of the animal soul debate, the more strongly are we reminded of arguments and issues that have not yet become merely historical.[37]

More than three hundred years after the deaths of Descartes and Géraud de Cordemoy, psychologists are still struggling with problems related to the mind-body enigma. In Cordemoy's works one will recognize many of the implicit assumptions underlying much of psychology today, as well as numerous current theoretical conceptions. More important, perhaps, is a clear reflection of the close relationship between a theory of human nature and the particular intellectual context within which it was held and defended.

The availability of the present volume should contribute to an appreciation, not only for the conflicts surrounding views of the nature of man in the beginnings of modern science, of which psychology today is a part, but also an appreciation for the ingenuity demonstrated in encountering opposing points of view.

Finally, a few matters of historical interest should be noted which might account for Cordemoy's relative obscurity in the history of psychology.

Cordemoy's first work, *l'Action des Corps*, a discourse delivered at an assembly of one of the learned groups which formed to discuss important philosophical questions of the day, was printed in the 1664 edition of Descartes' *Monde*. Cordemoy's name did not appear on the publication.[38] Of further interest to the historian is information passed on by Cordemoy's recent biographers; they noted that the British Museum Catalog erroneously attributes *A Philosophicall Discourse concerning Speech . . .*, the first work reprinted in the present volume, to Louis-Géraud de Cordemoy, the son of Géraud de Cordemoy.[39] And, Cordemoy assumed the pseudonym "Des Fovrneilles" as author of the second work in the present volume. It was not uncommon for writers to use a pen name in the seventeenth century; those interested in the issues at the time had no difficulty identifying the author. Indeed, Cordemoy was a well-known figure in his lifetime. Rosenfield[40] wrote that Cordemoy was probably better known to the English public than any other defender of animal mechanism after Descartes and before Malebranche. Most likely Cordemoy's notability was due to the availability of the two works included in this volume in English translation.

In France, Cordemoy's intellectual milieu included most distinguished seventeenth century personalities; he was in high favor politically, served as the Dauphin's tutor, and was commissioned by Louis XIV to do a history of France.[41] He also served as Directeur of l'Academie Française.

Considering the scope and importance of Cordemoy's addenda to Descartes' philosophy, particularly his treatment of speech and thought, sensation and perception, it becomes important to place him among other notable figures in the history of psychology, and to make his writings more readily available.

BARBARA ROSS

University of Massachusetts—Boston

NOTES

1. A. G. Balz gives Cordemoy's birth date as 1600 (*Cartesian Studies* [New York, 1951]). P. Clair and F. Girbal document his year of birth as 1626 from Bibliothèque Nationale de Paris, MSS., *Dossiers bleus*, 210, cote 5327 (*Gerauld de Cordemoy Oeuvres Philosophiques* [Paris, 1968], p. 16.)

2. *Experimental Philosophy* (London, 1664; reprint. New York: Johnson Reprint Corp., 1966), p. 192.

3. Harvey delivered lectures before the College of Physicians in London from 1616 to 1618 in which he explained the discovery of the circulation of the blood. His book, *De Motu Cordis et Sanguinis*, was not published until 1628.

4. "Meditations," Reply to Objections IV, 1641. In E. Haldane & G. R. T. Ross, trans., *The Philosophical Works of Descartes* (Cambridge: At the University Press, 1967), 2:103.

5. *Le Discernement du Corps et de l'Ame en six discours pour servir a l'eclaircissement de la physique. Dediez au Roy* (Paris, 1666), Bibliothèque Nationale de Paris, R. 13654.

6. The original edition was written and published in 1668 in French as *Discours physique de la Parole. Dedié au Roy* (Paris, 1668). There were four editions in French, and a Latin translation in addition into the English. For a complete bibliography of the works of Cordemoy see P. Clair and Girbal, op. cit.

7. Jacques Rohault (1620–1675) was a close friend of Cordemoy and promoted similar views in *Treatise on Physics* (1671). He advocated the same science in-

spired by Cartesianism as put forth by Cordemoy. Although Rohault was considered one of Descartes' strongest supporters, he agreed that modification and clarification of Cartesian philosophy were needed.

8. Clair and Girbal, op. cit., p. 41.

9. For a detailed discussion of Cordemoy's anti-Cartesian ideas see Clair and Girbal, op. cit., pp. 39 ff.

10. F. A. Lange, *History of Materialism* (London, 1877), 1:254.

11. For Descartes' reply to Gassendi's objections to his "Meditations," see Haldane and Ross, op. cit., p. 123. Essentially, Descartes replied that he was unable to discover any points that needed his comments.

12. For a comparison of Cordemoy and Gassendi on the Cartesian treatment of matter see Clair and Girbal, op. cit., pp. 310, 312.

13. For Descartes' treatment of matter see Meditation VI in Haldane and Ross, op. cit., 1:196 ff.; also, 1:57 ff.

14. Ibid., pp. 116 ff.

15. If man reasons because of the possession of a soul, and if one asks, as Cordemoy did, if God gave similar souls to all men, how can differences in ability to communicate and understand be accounted for? The answer given by Cordemoy is that faculty of understanding comes from the brain; impressions are more easily received, better arranged, and make thoughts easier in the brains of some than others. The differences lie in bodily organization.

16. La Chambre (1594–1669) made a distinction between general and particular reasoning several years before Cordemoy's book was published, but the two varied in their views of man-brute differences. La Chambre distinguished between man's ability to form general concepts which was intellectual reasoning, and what he called "imaginative reasoning" of animals. By assigning reasoning of any kind of animals, he supported the anti-automatist view that animal intelligence was merely different in degree from man's. Cordemoy argues that animals are not different in degree from man, but are different in kind. He admits that animals sometimes exhibit behavior that *appears* to involve reason; his explanation, however, is that beasts react appropriately (and mechanically) simply through God's design. He also relies on "God's design" to explain man's rational behavior. For a detailed discussion of La Chambre's views, see S. Diamond, "Marin Cureau de la Chambre (1594–1669)," *Journal of the History of the Behavioral Sciences* 4 (1968) :40-54.

17. Fabri, a Jesuit who held a certain respect for the natural science of the seventeenth century, enthusiastically supported Cartesian dualism and animal automatism; however, he rejected Descartes' use of animal spirits as well as the Scholastic reliance on substantial form. See *Tractatus duo: quorum Prior est de Plantis et de Generatione Animalium; Posterior, de Homine* (1666), reviewed in *Phil. Trans.* (22 October 1966) : 325 ff.

The rationalism and mechanism of Descartes were promoted by Thomas Cornelius, but he insisted as well on the direct study of Nature itself, and qualified his approval of Cartesian mechanism. See *Phil. Trans.* (9 December 1667):576.

18. Original was in French: *Copie d'une Lettre Ecrite à un sçavant Religieux de la Compagnie de Jesus: Pour montrer, I. Que le Systeme de Monsieur Descartes, et son opinion touchant les bestes, n'ont rien de dangereux. II. Et que tout ce qu'il en a écrit, semble estre tiré du premier Chapitre de la Genese* (1668). Cordemoy

xviii

and Cossart frequented l'Academie Lamoignon, a group of intellectuals who met weekly to discuss primarily, the finer forms of literature. Note that Cordemoy took the pseudonym "Des Fovrneillis" in the *Letter*. . . .

19. For a review of this work, see *Phil. Trans.* 7 (22 April 1672):4054.

20. According to Sherrington (*Man on his Nature*, 2d ed. [Cambridge: At the University Press, 1951], p. 152), Fernel suggested ninety years before Descartes, that the pineal gland acts as a valve controlling the passage of animal spirits between the forward and hindward chambers of the brain.

21. "Passions of the Soul," Arts, XXXI-L, in Haldane and Ross, op. cit., pp. 345 ff.

22. Also, Nils Stensen: he was a colleague of Cordemoy's at l'Academie Bourdelot.

23. Steno gave the *Discourse* . . . in 1666, but it was not published until 1669. It was reviewed in the *Phil. Trans.* 4 (20 September 1669):1034 f. The *Discourse* . . . is available in reprint: G. Scherz, ed. (Copenhagen, 1965).

24. Scherz, op. cit., p. 97.

25. Pineal gland.

26. *Phil Trans.*, 2:480.

27. Scherz, op. cit., 140.

28. For a review see *Phil. Trans.* 13 (10 February 1682-83):62 ff.

29. Borelli was credited by Boring (*A History of Experimental Psychology*, 2d ed. [New York, 1950]) with introducing the concept of *succus nerveus* in a more material way than "animal spirits" had been used before. However, William Cole (1635-1716), a relatively obscure physician, published *De Secretione Animali Cogitata* in 1674 which was reviewed in the *Philosophical Transactions* (9:134 ff.); in that book, Cole claimed to establish the existence of the "nervous juyce" and the use of it in a way "not hitherto been taught by any, though some have assigned to it a *Fermentative* power, ..." His work, which focused on secretion, was very mechanical. Actually, Cordemoy, *before* Cole and Borelli uses the term "animal spirits" as a purely physical and physiological principle.

30. Evidence other than physiological contributed to the scepticism: cultural differences, and the discovery of fossils, for example, not accountable on the basis of traditional explanations were disconcerting; and the thesis of monogenetic origin seemed no longer adequate. Anti-scriptural solutions to the problem of man's place in nature were offered as some proposed that there were multiple kinds of men. Petty, in *Scale of creatures* (1676-77), provided an anti-scriptural account or solution to the place of the newly discovered savage in the universe; he suggested that some men had a natural place in the order of things and that their place was inferior to that of European man. Tyson (1650–1708) proved that apes were more closely related to man than to any other animal, and that the pigmy (in *Homo sylvestris*) was probably an ape-like creature.

31. *Discourse concerning speech* . . ., p. 123.

32. Ibid., p. 121.

33. F. Bouillier, *Histoire de la philosophie cartésienne* (Paris, 1854). Also, Cordemoy's use of "occasion" (à l'occasion de) is explained in the preface of *Le Discernement du Corps et de l'Ame en six discours pour servir, a l'eclaircissement de la physique* (Paris, 1666), and is developed in Discourses IV, V, and VI. That work has not yet been translated into English.

34. Published in 1674; available in reprint: See G. Lewis, ed. (Paris, 1946). For references to Cordemoy in Malebranche's work, see Clair and Girbal, op. cit., p. 369.

35. A. Vartanian, *La Mettrie's L'Homme Machine* (Princeton, 1960), 57 ff.

36. Ibid., p. 5.

37. Balz, op. cit., p. 149.

38. *Le Monde de Mr. Descartes ou le Traité de la lumière et autres principaux objets des sens, avec un Discours de l'Action des Corps et un autre des Fièvres, composés selon les principes du même Auteur.* (Paris, 1664.) Cordemoy's name did not appear on the publication; neither did Rohault's. The latter authored *Discours des fievres.* See Clair and Girbal, op. cit., p. 29.

39. Catalog No. 1135, b40. Clair and Girbal, op. cit., p. 5.

40. *From Beast-Machine to Man-Machine: Animal Soul in French Letters from Descartes to La Mettrie* (New York: 1941), p. 41.

41. Clair and Girbal, op. cit., p. 53.

A Philoſophicall
DISCOURSE
Concerning
SPEECH,

Conformable to the

CARTESIAN PRINCIPLES.

Dedicated to

The Moſt Chriſtian
King.

Engliſhed out of *French.*

In the *SAVOY*,
Printed for *John Martin*, Printer to the *Royal
Society*, and are to be ſold at the *Bell*, a
little without *Temple-Bar*, 1668.

1

TO THE

KING.

SIR,

This Difcourfe is the sequel of some others, that have already appear'd in publick, under the Auguft Name of Your MA JE-STY. I thought I was obliged to offer unto You the *Firft* part of this Work, forafmuch as having propof'd to my felf at the begining, to give each man to confider,

A 2   *what*

3

what He is , me thought, that Your MAJESTIE should find in this consideration more pleasure than all other Men. I have the same reasons to present this also to You, where I treat no more of the *Knowledge of our selves,* but of the *Means to know others,* and *to be known by them.* I shew, that this Means is SPEECH; I explain all the Effects thereof, and the better to discover the Causes, I carefully inquire into all, it borrows from the Body or the Soul. These Causes, SIR, are so excellent in Your MAJESTIE, that You will doubtless have an incredible satisfaction to examine them: A-bove all things I am perswaded, You will find more of it than any Man, when you shall consider its *Effects.* You will see, it is *Speech,*

which

which produceth what Your MA-
JESTY loveth moft, I mean,
Glory, and you'll acknowledge,
that to it you owe that Luftre,
which maketh Your MAJESTY
out-fhine all the Powers of the
Earth. 'Tis by it, SIR, that
You exprefs thofe Generous
Thoughts, which all tend to our
Felicity; and 'tis by the fame;
that you have atchieved thofe
great things, which make all Na-
tions fay, that *You* are the Greateft
Prince that ever was.

I know, SIR, that men admire
no lefs in Your MAJESTY the
Faculty you have to be filent, than
the Facility to fpeak : I know, I
fay, that the Prudence you have
to be filent, is one of the reafons,
which make others fpeak fo much
of *You*. But I remember very

A 4 well,

5

well, that *Secrecy*, how favorable
ſoever it is to great Deſſeins, cannot alone make them ſucceed, and
that, how-ever Your MAJESTY
hath advantagiouſly uſed it in all
the Contrivances you have made
for our Happineſs, you would never have obtain'd the Execution
thereof, if you had not employ'd
Speech; it was neceſſary, Orders
ſhould be given for that. Indeed,
SIR, you know how to give them
as becoms a Prince, who needs
none but himſelf to *contrive* and
to *reſolve*. You alone know, why
you give them, and thoſe that receive them, often not know the
excellent End, Your MAJESTY
propoſeth to your Self, but at the
moment, which makes them ſuc-
ceſfull.

How amiable is *Glory*, when a
Man

Man thus owes it entirely to himfelf! And how pure & fincere doth
that of Your MAJESTY appear
to me? Others, who have only
Power for their Portion, hear
themfelves praifed for a thoufand
Events, wherein their Conduct
had no part : Words are alwayes
found for them. But all the Actions of Your MAJESTY, are fo
much above what can be faid of
them, that thofe to whom Praife
cofts leaft, complain they can find
none to expreffe them. Such an
one hath demanded Ten *years* to
write, what we have feen *You* do
in Ten *dayes* : And another that
knows, it requires lefs pains to
compare *Hero*'s with one another,
than to write their Praife, hath endeavour'd to find like ones to Your
MAJESTY, but could meet with

A 4   none

7

none among all thofe, whom An-
tiquity hath left recorded. Indeed,
S I R, none of them are known,
whofe Paffions have not guided all
their Enterprifes : the world hath
feen him, whom paft Ages have
moft boafted of, to follow nothing
but the motions of his Ambition,
and, without at all confidering the
tranquillity of his Subjects, to carry the trouble into whole *Afia*;
whereas, S I R, all *Europe* hath
feen You, young and victorious,
fhewing favour to your Enemies,
that you might give Peace to
your people : And it feeth at this
very time, that *Your Majefty* co-
vets not a great Country expofed
to your Conquefts, but defires only
what of right you can pretend to.
This moderation, S I R, is the
greateft Virtue of *Kings*, and efpecially

cially is it admirable in a Prince *vi-gilant* enough to surprise the Ene-my in a season, when the most ar-dent Spirits for war, do quit that painful exercise ; and *brave* enough to execute himself, what the bold-est durst not advise. What Mor-tals, SIR, could have stopt *Your Majesty*, accomplisht with these Excellencies, if the Right of *Bien-seance* could have tempted you ? But your Neighbours were to as-sure themselves afresh,'tis not Am-bition that hath armed you ; 'tis from the hands of Justice, you hold that sword, which subjects the *Provinces* in less time, than needs to march through them. *Brabant* and *Henaut* may give te-stimony hereof to the rest of the World. *Your Majesty* hath made them know your Right, because you

9

you let them feel the force of your
Armes; and 'tis known, that their
Revolt is the only cauſe of thoſe
great Exploits, which Hiſtory will
never be able ſufficiently to cele-
brate, and for which *Poeſie* it ſelf,
which boaſts to ſpeak like the
Gods, confeſſes to want expreſſi-
ons. But *Sir*, though *Poeſy* cannot expreſs the ſurpriſing effects
of your Courage, take it in good
part, that *Philoſophy* does rebuke
the *Exceſs* of it, and that with her
uſual liberty ſhe reproaches you for
having expoſ'd your *Sacred Perſon*
like that of a Common Souldier.
This reproach would make up the
Glory of every other Prince; but
Sir, how could any man have ex-
cuſ'd *You* to poſterity, if that
Great Heart, which is not given
you but to ſuſtain the Deſtiny of
France,

France, had made you be cast away in this occasion? One cannot praise enough this ardor, which maketh you quit pleasures in the midst of Winter; but how noble soever it be, it is to be blamed, when it makes you seek dangers, and when it exposeth, against *rebellious* Subjects, a life so precious to so many other faithful ones. Be pleased, *Sir*, to hearken to that zeal, which speaks to you; It hath alwayes lov'd Kings, it hath never flatter'd them, and as it knows none greater than *Your Self*, it cannot at that time, when it intends to discourse of *SPEECH*, make better use of it for the good of the Universe, than to tell what you owe to your own *Preservation*.

I shall add, *Sir*, that the same being

being to declare it self upon this
Subject by the mouth of a *Man*, it
could not choose any one, whose
Zeal were equal to mine. I am

SIR,

Of Your Majesty

*The most humble, most obedient,
and most faithful Servant
and Subject,*

CORDEMOY.

The

The Preface.

I Propoſed in the Six Diſcourſes, which preceded this, * the means to know Our ſelves, & made it manifeſt, that it only conſiſted in diſcerning in us the Operations of the Soul, and thoſe of the Body. Now I propoſe the means of knowing Others, and that is SPEECH. I explain as far as I am able, What it is; and pourſuant to my firſt deſſein, I endeavour in this Diſcourſe exactly to diſtinguiſh what it borrows of the Soul, from what it holds of the Body.

*Publiſht A. 1666. under the Title, Le diſcernement du Corps & de l'Ame; of which ſee Phil. Tranſ. No. 17. p. 306.

I. To begin this Inquiry with the more certainty, I do not reaſon but upon what I have found within my ſelf in the Sixth Diſcourſe of the lately mentioned Book; and as if I had never yet been aſſured, there

were

13

were other *Men* besides my *self*, *I stay in the very beginning upon this Considera-tion,* viz. Whether it be neceſſary, that all the Bodies, which I ſee to be like mine, be united to Souls like mine? *Re-ſolving with my ſelf not to believe it, un-leſs I have ſuch evident ſignes thereof, that I may doubt no more of it. I examine, what thoſe Bodies do that's moſt ſurpri-ſing; and as long as I can rationally impute the Cauſe thereof to the* Diſpoſition of their Organs, *I think, I may ſafely af-firme, they have no Soul. But after ha-ving found in the ſole* Diſpoſition of the parts of thoſe *Bodies, that thence I can render a reaſon of Noiſe, the Sounds, the difference of the Voices, and the very Words utter'd by* Echo's *and* Parrets, *I am at length obliged to admit Souls in all the Bodies that reſemble mine, and to ac-knowledge it not poſſible for them to ſpeak to ſuch purpoſe, as they do, without being endowed with* Reaſon.

2. *Next, having found, That to ſpeak is in general nothing elſe, but to* Give *ſignes of our* Thoughts, *I obſerve ſome of thoſe ſignes. The firſt, I conſider, are* the

The Preface.

the *Motions of the Eyes or Face*, *and such Cryes*, *as ordinarily accompany the differing states of the Body* : *And I take notice, that they are naturally conjoyn'd with the Passions, of which the Soul is sensible on the occasion of changes in the Body*; *and that the best way we have to manifest what she suffers*, *is, not to strain the Face, Eyes or Voice. I note likewise, that this way of explicating our selves, is the first of Tongues, and the most Universal*, *there being no Nation but understands it : But I observe at the same time, that the Wickedness of Men hath made that the most deceitful of all. Besides those Natural signes of the Passions of the Soul, I discover others, which are but Instituted ones, by which she can express what ever she conceives. I show briefly the agreement and the difference of some of those signes, to make all to be understood, what I intend to deduce from thence in this place; And reserving to my self to discourse of it more strictly, and more to my purpose thereafter, I stay to consider, How one may invent a Language*; *How a man may learn the Tongue of a Country, where no body understands*

The Preface.

derstands his ; and lastly, How Children learn to speak. I admire, how their Reason is put to it in that Infant-age, to make them discern and distinguish the signification of every word; above all, the Order, which they follow for that purpose, appears to Me surprising, forasmuch as 'tis altogether like that of the Grammar ; so that seeing, how much this Art imitates Nature, I find no difficulty to make it out, How those, that have given us the Rules thereof, have learnt them from little Children. And in this whole research I meet with so many Arguments to evince the Distinction of the Body and Soul, that to me it seems not, there can any thing be more evidently known, than She.

3 After some reflexions on so important a Truth, I betake my self, for the yet better knowing of the nature of Speech, to unfold in this place all what is to be found in it on the score of the Body. I consider therefore in him that speaketh, the manner how the Air enters into the Lungs; Why it maketh a sound in issuing out at the Wind-pipe? How the Muscles, that serve to open or shut this conduit, diversifie the sound?

16

sound? What parts of the mouth are em-
ployed to determine it in a Voyce? What
is the configuration of every one in these
different terminations? and what is the
Change of the Throat, the Tongue, the
Teeth, and the Lips, in all the Articula-
tions? Which giveth me to understand, as
much as needs, what Speech is, as far as
it depends upon the Body. I observe with
the same accurateness the effect, which by
sound is produced in the Ear and Brain
of him, that heareth. I find, it is from
the correspondency between the Brain and
the other parts of every Animal, that it
can be so differently moved by different
sounds; and examining chiefly the use of
the Nerves, which diffuse themselves
from the Ear to all the parts serving to
form the voice, I discover the reasons of
many odd effects, and amongst them, of
certain Birds imitating the singing of o-
thers, and the sound of our Musical In-
struments, and often our very Words.

4. I also draw from thence a convincing
argument, that Brutes need no Soul to cry,
or to be moved by Voyces, or even to imi-
tate the sound of our words; and that if
the

the cry of those, that are of the same Species, disposeth them to approach one another, and maketh those that are of a different kind, to retire; the cause of that is to
be sought no where else but in their Bodies
and the different construction of their Organs. But at the same time I find, that
in Men, the motion of the parts, which
serve for the Voyce, or of those that are
moved by it, is ever accompanied with
some thoughts; and that in Speech there
are alwayes two things, viz. the Formation of the Voyce, which cannot proceed
but from the Body; and the Signification
or the Idea, that is joyn'd therewith,
which cannot come but from the Soul.

5. And because hitherto I have said
almost nothing of the Voice, of Writing,
and of Signes, but what may serve to declare what those three Wayes of expressing
our thoughts have common (there having
been no occasion, sooner to observe the differences of each) I take notice in this place
of three sorts of Signes, of two sorts of
Writing and of two of Voices. I stay
principally upon the last, on which occasion
I finish the explication of what the order
of

The Preface.

of the precedent matters had not permitted me to explicate sooner, touching the easiness or difficulty, there is in joyning certain Idea's to certain Words, *when we learn a Language : And making out as accurately as I can, how all that is done, I find, that the trouble which some have to* conceive, *or to* explain *themselves, is not an imperfection in the Soul ; and that that marvellous facility, which others enjoy to express themselves, proceeds only from an happy Disposition of the Brain, and of all the parts that serve for the Voyce or for the Motions of the Body.*

6. *On which occasion I inquire into the natural causes of* Eloquence, *and find, that to the perfection thereof are required two talents at once, which by birth are never given to one and the same person, but yet that one of them being furnisht by* Nature, *the defects of the other may be supply'd by* Art. *And having remarked, that that is not reciprocal, I declare (as far as I may in a Discourse where I am to explain but the* Principles*)whence those defects proceed, and by what they may be corrected ; and I do even examine, without stepping*
into

The Preface.

into the Ethicks, *why an* Orator *ought to be a* good man, *and how much* Lying *may impair the force or the grace of his action.*

7. *Lastly, having considered sufficiently, how much* Eloquence *depends from the* Temperament, *and how it may be corrected or perfected by exercise, I examine, whether it is to be met with among* Spirits *not united to Bodies :* Which obliges *me to enquire into the manner, after which they may manifest their thoughts to one another ; and it makes me discover, that even* our Spirits *would enjoy a more easie communication among themselves, if the strict* Union *they have with the* Body, *did not indispensably oblige them to make use of* Signes. *The same raciocination teaches me also, that the difficulty we meet with in entertainments, is not to conceive the* thoughts *of those, that speak to us, but to unwrap it from the* Signes *they use to express it in, which often do not sute with it :* Whence *I conclude, that the Thought of one* Spirit *is alwayes clear to another from the very instant he can perceive it.* And *this truth (which I discuss as far as*

I

20

The Preface.

I am capable) serves me to resolve those difficulties, which others have thought unsurmountable but by submission to Faith. *I well know, 'tis* Faith, *that must teach us, whether sundry things have a being indeed; but there is not alwayes need of its aid to* conceive *them. It belongs to it, for example, to tell us, whether there be other* Spirits *more enlightned, that serve to direct ours; but when once it hath declared to us that truth, me thinks, our* reason *can attain to it. And I esteem, that reflecting a little on what the thred of my subject hath obliged me to write of it in this* Tract, *we shall find it more easie to conceive, how pure* Spirits *can inspire us with their sentiments, than to conceive, how one* Man *can inspire his thoughts to another.*

I might have proceeded further in this Inquiry, *but having proposed to my self only to examine what serves to* Speech, *I thought I was to make an end, after I had consider'd the sundry wayes by which* Thoughts *may be communicated, seeing that that is properly, what we call To* 'peak. *I could wish, that the discourse I*

have

have made of it, might prove as pleasant
to others as the reflexions, it hath obliged
me to make, have been to me. I avow,
they have been all the divertisement I
have enjoyed during the last Vacations,
and as it is, at least in that time, permitted to comply with our inclinations, the
pleasure I have found in it, sollicits me
strongly to spend in the same manner all
the other hours, wherein I may be permitted to divert my self. To conclude, this
Argument is so pleasant and so fertile,
that one needs but to propose it, and it will
beget a thousand pleasing thoughts : And
I doubt not, but all those that excell me in
genius, will find by occasion of this Discourse a thousand pretty things, which I
have omitted; so that without boasting of
my Book, I may affirm, that the more
Wit a man hath, the more pleasure he will
find to read it.

A

A
DISCOURSE
OF
SPEECH.

Mongſt the Bodies, I ſee
in the World, I perceive
ſome, that are in all
things like mine; and I
confeſs, I have a great
inclination to believe,
that they are united to Souls, as mine is.
But when I come to conſider, that my
Body hath ſo many operations diſtinct
from thoſe of my Soul, and that nothing
of what maketh it ſubſiſt depends at all
from Her, I think I have at leaſt ground

B   to

to doubt, that those Bodies are united
to Souls, until I have examin'd all their
actions : And I do even see, that by the
maximes of good sense I shall be obliged
to believe, that they have no Soul, if
they do only such things, whereof I
have found in my self that the Body a-
lone may be the cause.

Thus if I see, that the Objects make
different impressions on them by the
Eyes, Ears, Nose or Touch, and if I see
them eat, sleep, wake, feed, breath,
walk, and dye, nothing of all that ought
to make me believe, that there is any
other thing in them but a certain disposition of organs and parts, which indeed
is admirable, but yet so dependent from
the course and order of the other matter, that I have acknowledged *that* to
be the only cause in me of Nutrition,
Sleep, Respiration, and of the power,
which objects have to move the Brain
so many surprising wayes.

'Tis true, I have observ'd, that certain Thoughts always accompani'd in
me most of the motions of my Organs;
but yet 'tis true also, that by the exactest
pre-

precisene{s}, with which I have distin-
gui{s}h't what was in all my operations
on the account of the Body, and what
on the {s}core of the Soul, I have found
manife{s}tly, that if I had nothing but
the Body, I might have all what appears
to me in the other Bodies, which re{s}em-
ble mine.

It behoves me therefore to ob-
{s}erve tho{s}e Bodies neerer, and to examine, whether I may not perceive by
any of their Actions, that they are ru-
led by Souls. I {s}ee, that ordinarily they
are carried to places, where the Air
{s}eems mo{s}t proper to entertain by re-
{s}piration a due temper in the Bloud.
I {s}ee, that they withdraw likewi{s}e from
places, where the Cold might too much
retard the motion, and from tho{s}e,
where the Heat might render it too
quick. I {s}ee, that they often flye with
vehemence from the encounter of many
other Bodies, that appear to me of a
Shape and Motion capable to de{s}troy
them; and I {s}ee al{s}o, that they approach
tho{s}e, which may be beneficial to them:
And all the{s}e actions appear to me to

B 2 be

be done with a difcerning fuch as I find in me, when I do the fame actions.

Mean time, when I reflect, that I have found by other Contemplations, that the fole *Difpofition* of the *Organs* is the caufe of all thofe operations in me, I fear I affirm too much, if I attribute the different motions of the Bodies, that furround me, to another caufe, than to the agreement, there is between their Brain and the Objects; and then, as long as I do not fee them do but what is for their good, as to eat, to drink, to feek after coolnefs or warmth, and whatever may maintain them in a ftate futable to their nature, I am not to believe, there is any other thing in them but the *Organs,* which may fuffice for that.

But me-thinks, I fee them often do things that relate not at all to themfelves, nor their prefervation : I fee fome of them that meet with other Bodies, the encounter whereof muft in all appearance deftroy them : I fee even fome of them quit the food they need, and the places that fhelter them from what may

may be noxious to them, to run thither, where their deftruction is in a manner certain : And that makes me reafonably prefume, that in fuch occafions they may be guided by fomewhat, that is very differing from themfelves. For when I fee, that they approch refolutely to what is deftructive to them, and a-bandon what may preferve them, I cannot afcribe thofe effects to this Mechanical proportion or agreement, that is between them and the Objects : And fince I have often noted, that notwitftanding the bent my body hath towards certain things, and that in fpight of the force, wherewith its ftructure makes it avoid others, I have yet a will *contrary* to its natural difpofition, which makes it often to be tranfported after a manner quite differing from that, it would be, if it follow'd nothing elfe but the difpofition of its organs, and the force which the objects exercife upon it; I can hardly keep my felf from believing, but that the motion of all the Bodies, that refemble mine, depends from a will like mine.

B 3 In

In a word, I can scarce doubt of it, when I reflect on the chain of many of their actions, that have no relation at all to what can preserve them; and above all, the connexion, I find between the *Words*, I hear them utter at all times, seems to demonstrate to me, that they have *Thoughts*. For although I do very well conceive, that a meer Engin might utter some words, yet I understand at the same time, that if the organs, which should distribute the wind, or open the pipes, whence those voices should issue, had a certain settled order among them, they could never change it, so that when the first Voice were heard, those that were wont to follow it, would needs be heard also, provided the wind were not wanting to the Engin; whereas the words, which I hear utter'd by Bodies, made like mine, have almost never the same sequel. On the other hand I observe, that those Words are the same, which I would use to express my thoughts by to other subjects, that should be capable to conceive them. Lastly, the more I observe the
effect,

effect, which my words produce, when I utter them before those Bodies, the more methinks that they are understood: and those, which they utter, answer so perfectly to the sense of mine, that there appears not any more ground to doubt, but that a soul performs that in them, which mine doth in me

Notwithstanding, in pursuance to that firme resolution, I have taken to admit nothing in my belief, but what shall appear evident to me; after I have considered it enough, not to need to fear, I deceive my self; I will more seriously than ever reflect upon all what serves for *Speech*, since that is the surest way, I have, to know, whether all the Bodies, which so perfectly resemble mine, are indeed Men as I am.

The first, which seems to me worthy consideration, is, that there are many Bodies, that can cause a noise by impelling the Air, and that that noise may be different, according to the different concourse of Bodies, or the diversity of their parts: In which regard 'tis so far,

B 4 there

there fhould be need of fuppofing Souls
in Bodies to produce that effect, that
on the contrary I know, that the Noife
not happening but becaufe the Air is im-
pelled, the caufe of it cannot rationally
be imputed but to what is capable to
impel it, that is, to a Body.

I know alfo, that by the aid of *Mechanicks* one may fo fitly adjuft certain
Bodies to one another, that they fhall
be able to compofe inftruments capable
to make agreeable founds, and even to
imitate the Songs, which I have fometimes ufed to exprefs grief or joy.

I know further, that Rocks and other
like Bodies can make us underftand not
only Sounds, as Mufical Inftruments do,
but alfo Words perfectly articulated.
'Tis true, I know, that they form them
not, and that, as they would repel a ball
to him that fhould caft it on them, they
do no more but fend back the words to
him that hath utter'd them, that is, they
drive back to him the fame air that was
driven to them, without changing any
thing in that impreffion; which maketh it carry the words fo far from the
places,

30

places, where they are pronounced, when there is nothing to ſtop them.

I conceive likewiſe, as I have already ſaid, that *Art* may go ſo far as to frame an Engin, that ſhall articulate words like thoſe, which I pronounce; but then I conceive at the ſame time, that it would only pronounce thoſe, that were deſign'd it ſhould pronounce, and that it would always pronounce them in the ſame order.

So that I ought not haſtily to believe, that whatſoever can make a Noiſe, render a ſound, form voices, or pronounce words, hath *Thoughts*; and I ought, above all, to take notice, that the wonderful Workman, to whom I owe the ſtructure of my Body, hath ſo mechanically diſpoſed and order'd all the parts, and principally thoſe that ſerve for the voice, that to form *it* I need no Soul: The ſole motions of the Muſcles, the Breaſt and the Diaphragme can make the Air enter into my Lungs, or let it out; and the only ſcituation of the artilages of the *Larynx*, diverſly changed by the ſmall Muſcles which ſerve to move

B 5, them

them, may be the cause of a thousand sharp or grave sounds, sweet or shrill, piercing or weak, according to the different flexures, the air receives in that passage.

I ought also to consider, that when I articulate divers words, it is only because that the Air, which is already let out of the throat, is diversly agitated, according as the Muscles of my Tongue move the same either upwards or downwards in my mouth; or else because being near to get out, it is agitated according to the different ways; in which my Teeth or my Lips can apply themselves to one another by the motion of *their* Muscles.

Besides I must consider, that the Muscles, which serve to move all those parts, are not moved themselves, but according as my *Brain* is agitated, and that that can be so, a thousand different ways by the *Organs* of *Hearing* ; my soul having no other part in all those motions, but to perceive the effects thereof.

Lastly, I am to take notice, that there
is

is fo great a communication and corre-
fpondency between the Nerves of the
Ear, and thofe of the *Larynx*, that
whenfoever any found agitates the
Brain, there flow immediately fpirits
towards the Mufcles of the *Larynx*,
which duely difpofe them to form a
found altogether like that, which was
juft now ftriking the Brain. And although I well conceive, that there needs
fome *time* to facilitate thofe motions of
the Mufcles of the Throat, fo that the
Sounds, which excite the Brain the firft
time, cannot be eafily expreffed by the
Throat, yet notwithftanding I doe as
well conceive, that by virtue of repeat-
ing them it will come to pafs, that the
Brain, which thereby is often fhaken in
the fame places, fends fuch a plenty of
fpirits through the nerves, that are in-
ferted in the Mufcles of the Throat, that
at length they eafily move all the cartilages, which ferve for that action, as
tis requifite they fhould be moved to
'form Sounds like thofe, that have fhaken the Brain.

Thus it is not enough, that Bodies
make

33

make Sounds, form Voices, and even
articulate Words like those, by which
I express what I think, to perswade me,
that they *think* what-ever they seem to
say. For example, I ought not be so
rash as to believe, that a *Parret*
hath any *thought*, when he pronounces
some *Words:* For besides that I have
observed, that after having repeated to
him exceedingly often the same words
in a certain order, he never returneth
but the self same words, and in the same
coherence; It seems to me, that since
he does not make these returns to purpose, he imitates men less, than Echo's
doe, which never answer but what
hath been said to them; and if there
be any difference between Parrets and
Echo's, it is, that *Rocks*, tossing back the
Air without changing at all the impressions, it hath received, render the same
voices, that have struck them; whereas *Parrets* form another voice like that,
which hath struck the ear, and often repeat words, which are said to them no
more. But in short, as I cannot say,
that Rocks speak, when they return
words,

words, fo I dare not affirm, that Parrets fpeak, when they repeat them.
For it feems to me, that to *fpeak,* is not
to repeat the fame words, which have
ftruck the ear, but to utter others to
their purpofe and futable to them. And
as I have reafon to believe that none of
the Bodies, that make *Echo's,* do *think,*
though I hear them repeat my words,
feing they never render them but in the
order, I utter'd them in; I fhould by
the fame reafon judge, that *Parrets* do
not think neither.

But not to examine any further, how
it is with Parrets, and fo many other Bodies, whofe figure is very different from
mine, I fhall continue the Inquiry,
which I need; to know the *inward* con-
ftitution of thofe, who refemble me fo
perfectly *without;* and for that purpofe
I think, I may, after the difquifition I
have been making of all what caufeth
noife, founds, voices, and words, eftablifh
for a Principle,

*That if the Bodies, which are like
mine, had nothing but the facilnefs of pronouncing Words, I fhould not therefore believe*

35

lieve, that they had the advantage of be-
ing united to Souls : But then, if I finde
by all the Experiments, I am capable to
make, that they use speech as I do, I shall
think, I have infallible reason to beleive
that they have a soul as I.

To make this examen in such an
order, as leaves me no suspicion at
all to have deceived my self, I must
consider before all, what I mean by
SPEECH. To *speak* (in my opinion)
is nothing else, but to make known
what we think to that creature which is
capable to understand it. And supposing that the Bodies, which resemble
mine, have Souls, I see, that the only
means to express to one another what
we think, is, to give to our selves external signes thereof.

But, me thinks, I have found, that
there are many signes common to them
and me, by which we understand one
another : for seing that they answer to
my signes by other signes, which give
me images agreeable to what I think, I
do not believe I am deceived, when I
perswade my self, that they have understood

flood my thought, and that the new thought, which their signes have excited in me, is really that, which they have.

Moreover, I see, I can agree with some of them, that what commonly signifies one thing, shall signifie another, and that this succeeds so, as that there are none but those, with whom I have agreed about it, that appear to me to understand what I think.

Whence I conceive, that those *signs* are of *Institution*, and as that *Institution* necessarily supposeth reason and thoughts in those, that are capable to agree about it, I should, it may be, advance nothing rashly, if I *now* affirmed, that those Bodies are united to Souls.

But that, which might trouble me here, is, that if there be *signs* of *Institution*, I think, I know others, that are alltogether *natural*. For example, all those, by which I express my passions without any design to do so : Thus a smiling Meen, and certain motions of my eies, or of the other parts of my
Face,

Face, make me often confider, when I confult with the Looking-glafs, that if others faw me, they would know my fadnefs, my joy, or the other paffions ftirring in me: And that, it may be (If thofe bodies refembling mine, have Souls) is the fureft means to difcover to them the different conftitutions of my Soul.

Yet, if I take good heed, I can render thofe figns very deceitful. For I find, that though naturally I appear outwardly chearful or fad, when I am fo indeed, yet I have the power to conftrain the motions of my face and eyes, fo as to make them have an Air quite differing from that, which they would have, if I left their motions free: Which gives me to underftand, that though naturally certain motions of my face, and even of my whole Body have been joyn'd to fome of my *thoughts*, yet this conjunction is not fo neceffary, but that I can fometimes alter it, by joyning thofe thoughts to other motions. And though indeed, that give me much pain, yet I conceive, that

that as we may form an easy habit of what at first appears very difficult, I could also render these changes easy enough to me.

But, what I am most of all to observe here is, that, although it be very convenient, that, as long as my Soul is united to my Body, (for the conservation whereof she hath divers passions) her joy, her sadness, her desires, or her fear be alwayes joyn'd with the motions, which the good or ill disposition of that Body can beget in the Brain; as also that that correspondence which is between the parts of the Brain and those of the Face or Eyes, and all such as are external, be the cause, that what is *within*, may never change, unless there be marks of it *without*; yet notwithstanding, since those exteriour marks have no necessary relation but to the changes of the Brain, and that the sole condition of the Body may be the cause thereof, it might happen, that though the Bodies, which resemble mine, should not be united to Souls, that yet they would have the same motions of eyes and

and face, which I often perceive in me,
according as they should be well or ill
dispos'd within ; so that those external
signes, so like in those Bodies and mine,
are not alone an infallible argument,
that those bodies are endow'd with
Souls.

Further, since those motions of the
face and eyes, and even those cryes,
that are never wanting, when nothing
constrains them, to follow the different
conditions of the Body by reason of the
relation, there is between all the parts
thereof, may very properly be call'd the
natural signes of the State, the Body is
in; I shall be careful to forbear, when
the eyes and face, or even the Cryes of
those Bodies shall not appear to me excited but by the objects, that may benefit or hurt them, to believe, that those
external motions are the signs of any
Thought.

But yet, when I shall see, that those
Bodies shall make signes, that shall have
no respect at all to the state they are
in, nor to their conservation : when I
shall see, that those signs shall agree
with

with thofe which I fhall have made to exprefs my *thoughts* : When I fhall fee, that they fhall give me *Idea's*, I had not before, and which fhall relate to the thing, I had already in my mind : Laftly, when I fhall fee a great fequel between their fignes and mine, I fhall not be reafonable, If I believe not, that they are fuch, as I am.

Thus I have no more caufe to doubt concerning this point ; for I have many a thoufand like tryals, and I have not onely feen a great connexion between their *figns* and my *thoughts*, but I have alfo found fo great an one between *their* fignes and *mine*, that I can doubt no longer of their *thoughts*. And if the power, I have to hinder, that the exterior motions of my face, and the other fignes of my paffions may not exprefs them, hath been one of the reafons, I have had to acknowledge, that my thoughts were very different from the motions, that are wont to accompany them ; I can now affure, not onely that thofe other Bodies, which refemble mine, have *thoughts*,
but

but alfo, though they can, as I my
felf, not let them alwaies be *fo* joyned to
the motions, which ufe to fignifie
them, that one ought alwaies to truſt
them; Yet I have found, that they
knew the art of conſtraining themfelves, and frequently after many figns
on their fide, and mine, which fhew'd
me that they underſtood my thoughts,
and made me believe that I underſtood
theirs, I perceived, they had a deſign to
deceive me.

Now then. ſince I may doubt no
longer, that the Bodies, which refemble mine, are united to Souls, and in a
word, ſince I am aſſured, that there
are other men beſides my felf, I think I
ought carefully to inquire into what remains to know of *Speech*.

Hitherto I have diſcours'd of it but
in *general*, and faid only, that *To fpeak*
was to give figns of one's Thought:
But in regard that the little reflexion,
I have made on thefe fignes, hath already difcover'd to me fo important a
truth, and that I alfo fee, that thofe
                                    fame

same signes are the only means to entertain Society amongst Men, which is the greatest good, they have in this World, I intend as much as I can to observe the different sorts of them together with their properties, and to endeavour to discover all the wonders of them, to learn all their uses.

One of the chief things, I finde worthy of consideration touching these *signs*, is, That they have not any resemblance to the *Thoughts*, which men joyn to them by *institution*. And indeed, whether we express our thoughts by *gestures*, by *discourse*, or by *characters*, (which are the three sorts of the most used *signs*, by which we manifest our *thoughts*) we cannot but see (if we consider it with some attention) that there is nothing less resembling our Thoughts, than is all that, which serves us to express them. For, when a man, to declare that he agrees not with me in such or such a thing, is shaking his head, and when the better to express it, he moveth his throat, tongue, teeth and lips, to form words,

or

43

or takes paper and with a pen traces characters to write it to me, I see so little resemblance betwixt all those motions of the Head, of the Mouth, or of the Hand, and what they teach me, that I cannot enough wonder how they *so easily* give me the understanding of a thing, they *so ill* represent.

But what is most admirable herein, is, That this vast difference between those *Signs* and our *Thoughts*, doth by marking to us *that*, which is between our Body and Soul, teach us at the same time the whole Secret of their Union. At least methinks, that that strict union, which the sole Institution of men is able to settle betwixt certain external Motions, and our Thoughts, is to him that will consider it, the best means to conceive, wherein in truth consists the Union of the Body and the Soul. For certainly, if we do conceive, that men can by *institution* joyn certain Motions to certain Thoughts, it cannot be hard to conceive, that the Author of Nature, in forming a Man, so well unites some Thoughts of his Soul to
some

44

some motions of his Body, that those motions cannot be raised in the Body, but the thoughts must also be forthwith excited in the Soul, and that reciprocally as soon as the Soul will have the Body move after a certain manner, it be so at the same time.

For the rest, 'tis evident, that from this so necessary relation, which the Authour of Nature maintains betwixt the body and the soul, it is that that necessity of making Signs to express our thoughts hath its rise. For, seeing the Soul can have no *thought*, but at the occasion whereof there will be made a *motion* in the Body, and that also she cannot receive any *Idea* of what is *without* but by the motions excited *in* the Body, which she animateth; it must needs be, that two Souls united to two different Bodies do express their thoughts by *Motions*, or, if you will, by outward *Signs*. But to know perfectly, how that is done, there needs, in my opinion, to be made but a little reflexion on what I have already observ'd about the principal differences of Signs, on the particular

45

ticular caufe of each, and on the reafons, men have to ufe them.

And firft, if it be true, that certain
motions of the Face, and certain Cryes
do naturally follow certain conditions
of the Body by vertue of the relation,
which is between all the parts thereof,
we muft believe, that the thoughts,
which are naturally joyn'd to thofe motions of the Face, and to thefe Cryes,
are the paffions, which the Soul fuffers at the occafion of the State, the
Body is in ; fo that if a man hath
well obferved his Eyes, his Face, and
all the outward parts of his Body during the time he hath been in certain paffions, he hath been able, feeing
the fame motions in another man, to
Judg, that that man felt the fame paffions: 'Tis true, if at times he hath
been fo dextrous as to conftrain
himfelf in the like ftate, he may have
learn'd to miftruct thofe fignes; but ftill
'tis manifeft, that they are naturally
proper to declare paffions, and that the
beft means to make one underftand
what the Soul fuffers, is, not to conftrain

46

ftrain the Face, the Eyes or the Voice;
'tis the moſt natural way to expreſs
our thoughts; 'tis alſo the firſt of all
the Languages, and the moſt Univerſal
that is in the World, ſince there is no
Nation, but underſtands it.

There are two other wayes to expreſs not only the Paſſions of the Soul,
but alſo what ever ſhe conceiveth, *viz.*
Speech, and *Writing*; which, to ſpeak
truth, are but one and the ſame thing.
For, men having obſerv'd, that they
could form different *Voices* or different *Letters*, did agree, that the *words*
or the *Letters* ſhould ſignify *Things*,
and they expreſs'd themſelves by the
one or by the other of thoſe wayes,
according as it was more convenient
to the State, they were in; if they
were abſent, the *letters* which remain
after they are drawn were more convenient for them, becauſe they could
be carry'd where a *voice* could not;
but if they were preſent, words utter'd
ſeem'd to them a more facil way to expreſs themſelves; and laſtly, if there
were ſome, that had not the freedom

C   of

of the voice, he might by Characters
expose to the Eye the Signs of his
Thought: So that if there be any re-
al difference 'twixt *Writing* and *Speaking*, 'tis, that in *Speaking* we make use
of the *Voyce*, and in *Writing* of *Chara-
ters*, which 'tis true, are very differing
signs, but in both we express our selves
by things external and corporeal, which
by *institution* are made to signify what
we think; and that *in general* is what
we call *Speaking*.

This being so, there is no man, that
may not conceive, that one can *learn*
a Language, or a way of Writing, and
that one may even *invent* them. For it
is evident, that whether we learn them,
or invent them, we do nothing else but
agree, that certain *Characters* shall signifie certain thoughts. It appears also,
that if there be a difference between
learning and inventing them; it is, that
in *learning* them, we onely furnish our
selves with the signes, already agreed on
by other men, but in *inventing* them we
are Masters of the Institution, which
maketh that the *Words* or *Characters*
signi-

signifie rather one thing than another: And by this means it is, that almoſt all the Nations have made to themſelves different Languages.

But as 'tis eaſie to conceive, how men that ſpeak one and the ſame Language, may agree amongſt themſelves about the means of inventing new ones; I ſhall ſtay a while to conſider, how a perſon that hath no knowledge at all of the Language of a Country, may learn it, though thoſe of that Country ſhould know nothing of his.

For that end I conceive, that applying himſelf at firſt to know the names of the things, moſt neceſſary for *him*, he ſhould attentively hearken to all that ſhould be ſaid by thoſe, who ſhould hold in their hands, or ſhew any of thoſe things; and the word they ſhould repeat oftneſt in ſpeaking of that thing, being moſt likely the name of it, he ſhould, when he pronounces that word, at the ſame time, to obtain the thing, uſe ſome ſign to manifeſt he had need of it; and if, making that ſhow, and and giving to underſtand his need, he

C 2 ſhould

should not name it aright, men would
not be wanting to tell him the right
name of it; so that he might by the
like informations in a short time know
the name of many things, and how little
wit soever he had, observe, above all
things, the words that should be repeated to him oftnest, by answering to divers questions, he should make of the
name of the things, by pointing to them.
For, in all appearance, the words, that
should be found in all the answers nea-
rest the name of every thing, would
signifie, *That is called*, or *named*; so
that he would have no more to do but
to repeat *them*, for the making of new
questions.

When he shall have learnt by this
means the names of many things, he
might then, according as those things
should be beneficial or hurtful, observe
the words, which those, who should
manifest they were affected with them,
should use to express what they meant
by them, and by this way learn the
words, which signifying the *qualities*
are alwayes added to those, which signifie

50

nifie the things, to which those qualities belong.

Next, when he shall see done certain actions, *e.g.* of mounting, descending, going away, and coming, he might ask, *How that was called*, and when he shall know words enow to form discourses, wherein he might mingle *Verbs* with *Nouns*, that is to say, what he thought, concerning the things and their actions, he could then make himself to be understood, though he should as yet speak improperly as to the words and the construction.

But to see, that that is not impossible, we need only to consider, that such a thing must often happen to Travellers: And should not *Men of age* find means to make themselves to be understood in a Country where they come, since *little Children* find them to learn the language of the Country where they are born ? They bring nothing with them into the world, but what Nature gives to all men, to express pain, joy, or other passions : Mean while, *that* suffices them ; and how little time soe-

C 3 ver

ver they have lived, they so well study
the looks of their Nurse, that she can
make them weep or laugh, by only
looking on them. Thus they easily
know the passions of those that come
near them, by the external motions,
which are the natural signes of them.

They are somewhat longer to understand the *signes*, that men have *insti-*
tuted to signifie *things* ; but the need
they have of some of them, renders
them so attentive to all what is said of
those things, when they perceive that
they are touched or shewn by the hand,
that at length they learn the name of it.
'Tis true, that ordinarily we endeavour
to excite in them some passion (as joy)
by some cry, which accompanying the
shew that is made to them of the things
at the same time, when we tell them
their names, maketh that they are more
attentive to them, and by being more
affected with them by this means, they
retain them the better.

But in the taking pains to teach them
certain things, we often perceive, that
they know the names of a thousand
                                   other

other things, which we deſſeigned not
to ſhew them : And what is moſt ſurpriſing therein, is, to ſee, when they are
2. or 3. years of age, that by the ſole
force of their attention they are capable
to find out in all the conſtructions which
are made in ſpeaking of one and the
ſame thing, the name, we give to that
thing.

They learn after this, with the ſame
application and diſcerning, the words
which ſignifie the qualities of the things
of which they know the names.

At laſt, extending their knowledge
farther, they mark ſome actions or motions of thoſe ſame things; and obſer-
ving at the ſame time thoſe that ſpeak
of it, they, by virtue of their attention,
and hearing repeated the *words,* which
are mixt with the *names* that ſignifie the
things or their qualities, diſtinguiſh
thoſe that ſignifie action.

Thus a child of a ſtrong and vigorous
temper, ſeeing a Horſe that runs, ſeems
to have a mind to fly after it, thoſe that
intend to divert him, often asking him,
Whether he ſeeth the Horſe t And be-

C 4   cauſe

cause perhaps that word would be too
hard for him to pronounce, in regard
that Children do better pronounce all
the words, that need only the Lips or
the Gums to be well articulated, they
give him a name convenient for it ; and
when by the effect he maketh to get to
the Horse, he is come near the pronunciation of that word, he is led near the
Creature, which he is made to flatter,
by saying 'tis a fine, a good Horse :
which is often repeated as long as it suffers it self to be thus caress'd: But If the
Horse begin to stir or snort, which may
make one fear it might hurt the Child,
those that have a mind to take the
Child away from it, presently say, 'tis
a *naughty* Horse : And if that Child,
when 'tis carried away, expresseth by
crying it would stay, those that hold
it, fain a kind of fear, of which the
Child knowing the outward signes in
their looks, feels presently the like motions, which maketh it be contented to
be removed from the Horse : And
whereas during all that while the word
naughty is often repeated with demon-
strations

54

strations that make the Child more attentive, it conceiveth what this new
word means, remembers it, and often
repeats it his own way, so that, if after
such lessons the same Child sees an
Horse, it will repeat the word, which
signifieth to him that *Animal,* and if in
his approach to it he finds it gentle and
content to be stroaked, he names at the
same time the word that signifieth an
Horse, and that which signifieth its
gentleness ; but if it prance, the fear
which the Child will have of it, will
make it strive to get away, and to name
the word *naughty* as well as it can, after
that which signifieth an *Horse,* without
tying these two words together by any
Verb, that denotes any action.

I shall here mention on the by, that
'tis likely, that those who made the
Elements of the Grammar, made the
like Observations. As the whole art of
their method could not be deduced but
from the Nature it self, they must needs
have considered, how Children learn to
speak ; and I see that indeed *their* precepts are nothing but an Imitation of

C 5

those

those which Nature gives to Children.

First, *Grammarians* teach the *words,* that fignifie *things,* which they call *fubftantives;* then thofe that fignifie *qualities,* which they call *adjectives;* and till they have well diftinguifh't thofe two *names,* they teach not the words that fignifie the *actions* of things, which they call *verbs:* wherein they follow alfo the fons Nature gives to Children, who, as far as we can obferve, do not apply themfelves to hearken to the words which fignifie the *actions* of a thing, but when they already know the name of the *thing* it felf, and that of the *qualities,* which makes that thing pleafe or difpleafe them: for 'tis always according to this agreeablenefs, that they learn one thing rather than another.

And to explain that by the fame Example, which I have already begun to make ufe of; when the Child, whereof I have fpoken, knows well the name of the Horfe, and the names of the qualities, that make it pleafe or difpleafe him, the defire which it naturally hath

hath to extend its knowledge causeth it to observe the actions of the Horse when it sees it; and if at times we perceive, that following the *impetus* of its temper, it gives signs of joy, when it sees the Horse run, we shall then say with such out-cries as commonly do accompany Joy, and by moving the Child in a manner like that the Animal moves in, that the *Horse runs*; and this often repeated will make the Child conceive the word which expresses that *action*, insomuch that it will not fail to joyn the word, which signifies the *Horse*, to that which signifies its *action*.

We might, pursuing of the same example, shew, how a Child learns at length to speak a whole language; but 'tis sufficient to have exactly observed the beginnings of it, it being easie to understand the sequel thereof. That which is only to be noted here, is, that it requireth much more time to teach them the power of *Adverbs*, than the words that signifie *substances, qualities,* and *actions*, because it concerns not so much their conservation to know that

more,

more, or this *less* ; that *excess*, or this *defect*, which are express'd by the *Adverbs*, that are joyn'd to *things* , *qualities* or *actions*, as the *things*, *qualities* or *actions* themselves do.

It may also be consider'd, that when they begin to take notice of *the more*, *the less*, of the *excess* or *defect* ; they commonly express it by some motion, or some pointing at bigness, smalness, according as things touch one another strongly or slightly by their qualities or action.

'Tis the same with *Conjunctions* and o-ther *particles* invented to connect things, or to separate them. For, Chil-dren use them but seldom, and late ; be-cause they, following nature altogether, believe to have express'd the thing and its quality, when they have put the two words, that signifie them, to one ano-ther.

And the same a Child does as to the *action*, which he expresseth by putting the word, which signifieth it, next the name of the thing, without being yet able to discerne that preciseness of the *times,*

times,, or to obſerve that diverſity of *terminations*, which applying the word, that ſignifies one and the ſame action, to divers perſons and divers times, formeth *Conjugation*.

We might alſo ſhew, how a Child comes to know the *term* of actions, and laſtly we might draw from the natural order, wherein Children learn to ſpeak, notions to judge, which of all the Languages are the moſt perfect : For doubtleſs thoſe which we ſhould find in their ordinary conſtructions to follow moſt that *natural* order, ſhould paſs for the moſt perfect.

But ſince I only look here after the *Principles*, I am not to proceed ſo far to *particulars.* I deſire only, that by the way an important truth may be taken notice of, which this example of Children evidently diſcovers to us, *viz.* That from their birth they have their reaſon entire ; becauſe indeed this way of learning to ſpeak is the effect of ſo great a diſcerning, and of ſo perfect reaſon, that a more wonderfull one cannot poſſibly be conceived.

If

If in the sequel of age they appear without conduct, and almost without reason, it is to be consider'd, that 'tis the knowledge of affaires, and the matters they are to reason upon, which they want, rather than reason. To which may be added, that the Customs of the World, which make up all the wisdom of it, are often so contrary to what Nature, well order'd, would exact from men, that those who are born, need to live many years, to learn things so remote from what Nature teacheth. But alwayes 'tis manifest, that the Reason of Children is entire from the beginning, seeing they learn perfectly the Language of the Countrey where they are born, and that in less time than Men of age need to learn that of a Country, where they should chance to travel, and not find any body that understood theirs.

By this time it is not difficult to conceive, why 'tis so easie for us to learn a strange Language of a person that understands it, and understands also ours: For then we can easily enquire after the

name

name of every thing. By this means
also we may learn many Tongues, it being obvious, that after we have learnt
the word, which signifies a thing in
French, we may also learn, by what
words the *Italians*, the *Spaniards* and o-
ther Nations express that thing : And
what is remarkable, is, that when we
have once agreed, that many words
shall signifie one and the same thing,
we so well joyn the *Idea* or the thought
of that thing to each of those words,
that often we remember very well that
the *Idea* of it hath been given us, without remembring which of all those
words was employ'd for it : whence it
comes to pass, that when we are in company with persons of different Countries,
whose Tongues we understand,
we easily retain every news, and all
what was said upon the matters, that
were spoken of, without remembring
just the words nor the Language that
was made use of to give us those images,
which remain of them in us.

This also shews very clearly, me-
thinks, the distinction there is between
our

our *Thoughts*, and the *Words* whereby we express them : And as the principal end, for which I designed this Tract, is to shew this *distinction*, so I think I am not to omit in this place another Consideration, which, in my opinion, maketh *that* so evident, that 'tis not possible to doubt of it.

And that is, that when a man speaks in publick, and hath for his Auditors many persons of different Nations, the sense of his words is not apprehended but by those, who know the Language he useth, although the sound of his words do equally affect all the rest. But if the Soul were not distinct from the Body, and if *Thoughts* were not distinct from *Motions*, it would happen, that when the Brain of many persons should be affected in the same manner, they would all think the same thing at the same time, because they equally have what in that matter depends from the Ear and Brain. But because all have not agreed in this, that certain motions of those parts should signifie certain things, nor have joyned them to the images

they

they have of them, it happens, that one speaks fruitlesly of those things before them, and that they understand them not, though the words, employ'd to express them, strike their Ear and Brain, as they do the Ear and Brain of those that understand them.

The same thing may also be seen in those that study any Language. They often know in one instant the signification of a word, but know it no more in another, and yet they well remember the word; and they have also the image of the thing, which it is to represent to them; but they have not yet so well joyned the one to the other, that that image returns to their mind, when the word is pronounc'd which signifieth it.

Although I am perswaded, I have hitherto said nothing but what is grounded on principles clear enough to leave no doubt, and that possibly they might be sufficient to deduce other consequences from them, which might also discover to us some truths important enough; yet notwithstanding I believe,

that

that to clear up fully what remains to be
said, and even what hath been said already, it will be fit, before we proceed,
well to discriminate all, what is found
in *Speech* as depending from the Body,
from what there is in it, as depending
from the Soul; and then to consider
what it borrows from their Union.

Upon the account of the Body in
him, that forms the Voice, it is to be
consider'd, that he hath *Lungs*, into
which the Air enters by the Wind-pipe,
when the Muscles of the Breast distend
all the sides thereof by their motion;
just as Air enters in a pair of Bellows
at the end, when 'tis expanded by sepa-
rating the two sides thereof.

We are also to conceive, that as the
wind, which issueth out of Bellows,
when they are closed, would be capable
to thrust the Air as many different ways,
as we should put different pipes at the
place where the wind comes out; even
so the Air, which issues out of the
Lungs, when the Breast subsides, is diversly thrust, according as the Entry of
the Wind-pipe is differently disposed;
which

which I enlarge not upon, becaufe I
fuppofe, that 'tis generally known, that
befides many fmall griftly rings, ferving
to keep the fides of the membrane,
which forms that channel, by which the
Air enters into and iffues out of the
Lungs, from approaching one another
too near, there are three confiderable
ones, whereof one can fhut it felf fo
clofe, that when it is in that pofition, the
Air cannot get out of the Lungs but
with a great force. And fometimes alfo
it can fo enlarge it felf, as that the Air
may iffue out very eafily. But as between the greateft and the fmalleft A-
perture, of which it is capable, there is
an infinite diverfity of other Apertures,
of which every one makes a different
impreffion on the Air, we are not to
think it ftrange, that the Air which
comes out of the mouth, is able to make
fo many different effects.

I fuppofe alfo, that every one eafily
conceives, that the *Cartilage*, which
ferveth to modify the Air, is not defti-
tute of the mufcles, that are requifit to
open it, to fhut it, and even to keep it

in

in certain positions, as there shall be need to make one and the same sound last. These Muscles are disposed in so wonderful an order, that 'tis not possible to see it without admiration. The other two *Cartilages* have also their Muscles, and all things are so well ordered in that place, that one may raise or depress that Entrance, and open or close it, and that either slowly or swiftly, yet so that the motion of the small muscles, which serve for some of those actions, be not hindred by the motion of those, that serve for others: Which informs us, that 'tis from the sole disposition of that place of the *Wind-pipe*, that the difference of the sounds depends.

And 'tis to be observ'd, that if there were but that part, there would not be any difference betwixt the sounds, it would make, and those of a *Flute*, that is, it would make only uncertain sounds, and no voices: but to give them a *certain determination*, the *Mouth* is so fashion'd, that these sounds coming to be tun'd, receive different terminations according to the different wayes it opens.   If

If for example you open the Mouth as much as you can in crying, you cannot form but a voice in A. And for that reason the Character, which in writing denotes that voice, or termination of the sound, is called A.

If you open your mouth a little less, advancing the lower jaw towards the upper, you'll form another voice terminated in E.

And if you approach yet more the jaws to one another, yet without making the Teeth touch, you'l form a third voice in I.

But if on the contrary you go to open the Jawes, and at the same time draw the Lips together at the two corners, the upper and the lower, yet without quite shutting them, there will be form'd a voice in O.

Lastly, if you approach the Teeth, yet without quite joyning them, and at the same instant put out both the Lips by approaching them again, without quite joyning them, you form a voice in U.

It is so easie to conceive, how the motions that are given to all the parts of

of the Mouth in each of those formati-
ons of voices, being mixt, there may be
form'd voices, the termination whereof
shall be Intermediate between two of
those five voices; that I shall not stay to
examine how these middle or compounded Voices are form'd, which are
called *Dipthongues.*

But I believe 'tis necessary a little to
examine, how those motions of the
Voice are made, that make those different *Articulations* of it, which in writing are expressed by the Characters called *Consonants.*

Some are articulated by the Lips only; thus when we joyn our Lips without joyning the Teeth, we cannot form
the voice A, but in disjoyning the Lips
in such a manner, as makes us articulate
the Syllable *Ba,* whereof the *last* letter
expressing the termination of the Sound,
that is, the Voice, is called *Vowel;* and
the *first,* which marketh the manner
how this voice is articulated, sounding
together with it, is called H, *Consonant.*
Whence, by the by we may see, that
often the Voice may be good, without
being

being well articulated : For, the Lungs,
which thrust the Air, and the entrance
of the Wind-pipe, may be so well disposed as to make the Voice very agreeable and pleasing; but in the same person, who shall have that advantage, the
other parts of the Mouth may be so ill
disposed, that not being mov'd with
ease, nor corresponding the one to the
other with an intire justness, the Voice
shall not be well articulated.

What is said of B. with the Voice A.
may be said of the same *Consonant* with
other *Voices*, without any difference in
the articulation, which beginning alwayes with disjoyning the Lips is alwayes the same, and receives not its
different termination but from the different site, which the parts of the Mouth
put themselves in, to form those different Voices.

The *Consonants* P, and M. are formed
as B. by disjoyning the Lips; but with
this difference, that the Lips are to be
only joyned to pronounce B. by opening them; but they must be more
strongly closed and drawn inward to
utter

utter a P, and yet more closed and more drawn in, well to pronounce an M.

The Letter F. is utter'd by joyning the under-lip to the upper-teeth, whereas the former Consonants are form'd by joyning both Lips together.

The Consonant V. is pronounced as the Letter F. with this difference, that you do more press your Teeth against the Lip for the Letter F, than for the Consonant V.

The Letter S. is pronounced by approaching the Under-teeth near enough to the Upper-teeth, and the Tongue near enough to the Palat, not to let the Air pass, which is getting out of the Mouth, but by a kind of whistling: And the Letter Z. is pronounced after the same manner, only with this difference, that for Z. we leave a little more space to the air, by not approaching so much the Tongue to the Palat, and by so extending it that it may nearer approach the Teeth, than in the pronouncing of S.

D. is utter'd by an appulse of the top of the Tongue to the Gums of the upper-teeth; and T. by striking with
the

the top of the tongue against the place where the upper and lower teeth joyn.

As for the letter N. it is form'd by striking with the top of the tongue between the palat and the upper part of the teeth: And R. by carrying the top of the tongue to the upper part of the palat, so that the tongue being shaken by the air issuing forcibly, yields to it, and often returns to the same place, as long as one will have this pronunciation to last. And the letter L. is utter'd by carrying the top of the tongue between the place, where the letter N. and that, where R. is form'd.

G. is pronounc'd by a gentle appulse of the middle of the tongue to the inward extremity of the palat; and K. by its appulse to the same place with a little more force.

As to X, it is a pronunciation compounded of S. and K. For C, it may be said, that 'tis often pronounc'd like S. and frequently like K. The letter Q. is also pronounc'd like K.

Lastly, the J. *consonant* is pronounc'd by carrying the middle of the tongue

D   towards

71

towards the interiour extremity of the
palat, with lefs force than in G, when
'tis pronounced with an A, or O, or V,
For CH, it is a pronunciation of C.
joyn'd to a gentle afpiration; fo that
the fyllable *Ga.* comes from the bottom
of the Throat; the fyllable *Ka*, from
fomewhat more forward; the fyllable
Ja, from a place a little nearer the middle of the palat, and the fyllable *Cha*,
from the very middle of the Palat

I do not examine, why fome pronounce certain confonants better than
others.   For 'tis obvious, that the facility or difficulty of pronouncing comes
only from the difpofition there is in the
parts of the mouth, infomuch that if the
mufcles of fome of them be well difpofed, and thofe of others not, we fhall
pronounce the Letters well, where we
have need of the motion of the parts,
that are in a good difpofition ; and we
fhall pronounce ill thofe, where we have
occafion of the motion of parts , that
are difpofed ill. Thus little Children will
pronounce better the B. than P. D. and
fome others, where we need only the
lips

lips or some teeth, or the top of the
tongue, than those letters, to pronounce
which there is required the use of the
middle of the tongue, or where 'tis necessary to redouble the tongue to the
height of the palat, as the letter R ; because the humidity of their Brain maketh their tongue too thick : whence
we are wont, in speaking to them, to
alter the name of the things which they
knew first, when there are letters which
they cannot pronounce; and that a-
mongst Us, we mark to them their Father and Mother (*Pere & Mere*) by
words, of which the Consonants are
easie, being pronounced by the lips and
teeth, or by the tip of the tongue.

After we have taken notice as much
as was necessary, How *Sound* is form'd;
How 'tis terminated into Voices ; and
How articulated into syllables by him
that pronounceth (to consider nothing
but the *Body* ;) We are now to examine
the effect it produceth in the *Ear*, it
striketh, and in the *Brain,* it shaketh.

In regard that the *Anatomy* of the
Ear is a thing commonly known, and

that 'tis sufficient for every one to be persuaded in the *general*, that it is an Organ dispos'd to receive the air, when 'tis propelled by Bodies, which by touching one another drive it from betwixt them, or repelled by hard Bodies, or issuing out of the Lungs of an Animal; I shall make no description of it : I desire only it may be observ'd, that as many different shakings there are in the Air, so many different sorts there are of its passing into the Ear, and that according to those diversities it causeth a different agitation in the Membrane (stretch'd out in the bottom of the Ear) and in the Nerves answering thereto.

It may also be judged by what we know of the construction of Animals, even of Beasts, that according as the Agitation of the Nerves of the Ear is different, the Brain must be agitated in different parts; and likewise that 'tis always according as those different parts are agitated, that the spirits are differently distributed into the members.

But all that is perform'd by a necessary
ry

ry fequel of the mechanical difpofition
of the whole Body of every Animal,
and even of every Beaft, which being
of a certain kind, that is, made for one
thing or another, hath all what is neceffary to effect what the Author of
Nature propofed to himfelf in forming
it : It hath the Brain fo adjufted (according to its temperament) for all
what may conferve it, that if the Objects which can hurt it, move its Brain,
'tis alwayes after fuch a manner, which
maketh it to open in the places, whence
the fpirits may flow into the mufcles,
which ferve to make it retire from thofe
Objects; and if the Objects, which can
benefit it, move its Brain, 'tis alwayes
in fuch a manner, as maketh it to open
in the places, whence the fpirits may be
diffufed into the mufcles, which ferve
to make it approach to thofe Objects;
fo that if we fuppofe, that one and the
fame noife ftriking the ears of two
Beafts of differing kind, do agitate at
the fame time their Brains, we are to believe, that that agitation being diverfly
made in each, and in different parts of

D 3   their

their Brain, according as that which causes the noise, shall be agreeable or contrary to it, it will also happen, that the course of the spirits being necessarily different in those two Beasts, one of them shall be carried far from the object, whilst the other approacheth to it. Thus the howling of a Wolf may make a Sheep fly, but at the same time bring to him another Wolf.

But 'tis necessary to observe here, that although the Art, whereby the Brain of Animals is composed, be infinitely varied, and that 'tis admirable herein, that according to their different conformations 'tis always found so artificially disposed, that those Creatures must necessarily and according to all the rules of the Mechanicks approach to what is naturally good for them, and retire from what is naturally noxious to them; yet it was not possible, that within the small compass of their Brain there should be so many differing springs, that they could have a proportion necessary, and always well suited to all sorts of Objects.

But

But inftead thereof, their Brain is made of a fubftance foft enough, eafily to receive new impreffions, and yet confiftent enough to retain thofe,which in fome places thereof are made by certain objects, which being neither naturally good nor ill for them, do yet fometimes occafion confiderable benefit or mifchief to them; and frequently thofe traces, which at firft were not in the Brain, remain there fo well marked, that when the Objects, which cauſed them, prefent themfelves, the places, keeping the impreffion, being more agitated by them than the other, diffufe thence fuch fpirits into the mufcles, as ferve to carry the Animal nearer to or further from thofe Objects, according as they have been found beneficial or noxious to it.

Mean time, whereas there is much more danger for the Animal, to fuffer the approach of the Objects, that can hurt it, than there would be in the not approaching thofe that might do it good : at the time when there is yet no impreffion in its Brain at the occafion

of an Object, if then it happen, that
from a noise that Object begin to shake
the Brain of the Creature, it will never
fail to fly; especially if the Air hath
been agitated strongly, or in such a way
that hath troubled the Brain,

I believe there is no body, that hath
not often felt in himself the effects of
this surprise, and experimented how
much the Will, which the Soul then hath
to keep the Body in certain places, is
controled by this natural Disposition,
which maketh all the Spirits and Mufcles conspire together to transport it
far from thofe places, where a noise
is made; especially when 'tis so great,
that the whole Body is threatned to be
there destroyed.

Every one may also have found,
what force the agitation made in the
Brain by a noise not ordinary, hath to
make the Spirits, without one's thinking
on't, flow into the mufcles, that ferve
to transport the Body out of the places
where that noise happens.

But fince this is not yet the place proper to examine, what the *Soul's* part is
in

78

in *Speech*, we muſt, to finiſh the Obſer-
vations of what ſhe borrows from the
Body for the formation of a Voice,
call to mind a *Note*, I have already
made, which is, that the ſame Nerves
which anſwer to the Ears, have branches
ches going to the Teeth, the Tongue,
the Entrance of the Wind-pipe, and generally to all the places which ſerve to
form or modifie the Voice ; ſo that,
following Nature's Inſtitution, the ſame
ſhaking of the Auditory Nerves,
which affects the Brain with the motion, cauſed by a voice in the Air, is alſo
the cauſe, that the Spirits, which flow
from the Brain into the Nerves of all
the parts ſerving for the Voice, diſpoſe
their Muſcles in a manner, which an-
ſwering to the Impreſſion made by the
Voice in the Brain, puts them into a
ſtate to form a Voice altogether like it :
And if it have been neceſſary, that the
correſpondence, which is between the
Auditory Nerves and the Brain, ſhould
be ſuch, that when it ſhould be moved
by the concuſſions of the air, *that* ſhould
be done in different places of it accor-

D 5   ding

79

ding to the diversity of Noises, to the end that, following that diversity, the Spirits might diffuse themselves into the Muscles, that can carry away or stay the Animal, according as the causes of that noise are good or ill for the whole Body; It was no less requisite, there should be a sufficient commerce between the same Auditory Nerves, and those of the parts, that serve for the Voice, to bring it to pass, that when a voice should strike the ear, the Muscles of those parts might immediately be disposed as they ought to be, to form another perfectly like it.

And to manifest this necessity better, 'tis requisite to make two reflections. The *first* is, that if it concern Animals, to have their Brain shaken by the noise of certain Bodies, before they approach too near them, that so they may avoid them; it concerns them likewise to have their Brain moved by some other Bodies, to the end that they may be carried towards them, when they are remoter from them, than is requisite for their conservation, or conveniency.

The

The *other* is, that as, (confidering only each Animal according to its *species*) there is nothing more noxious to it, than thofe of a contrary *species*; fo there is nothing that can be more beneficial to it than thofe of its own kind.

That being fo, 'tis evident that nothing could be fo ufeful as this communication, which is between the Ears and the parts ferving to form the voice: For by this means the cry of one Beaft fhaking the Brain of another of its kind, it prefently comes to pafs, that not only it is carried towards that, which maketh the cry (according to what hath been faid) but befides, the Mufcles of its Throat do fo difpofe themfelves, that it makes at the fame time a like cry, and this new cry ftriking the Brain of that, which cried firft, caufeth the fpirit to flow into the Mufcles, which ferve to carry it toward the fecond; fo that they fooner meet, and may, according to the eaufes of the cry, that made them approach, draw from one another what may contribute to their confervation.

I

I very well know, that this necessity of forming cryes or voyces like those, that have struck the Ears, is not so universal, that it must so fall out always; and that there are two cases, wherein it happens otherwise even in Brutes.

The *first* is, when that Creature, whose Ear is struck, and whose Brain is agitated by a Cry, is not of *the same kind* with that which maketh the Cry. For we know, by what hath been above deliver'd, not only that the dispositions of the parts, which form the voice in Animals of different *species*, being altogether different, that cannot come to pass, but also, that what is the cause why a Brute makes a cry like that which is made by another of its own kind, is only that they may the sooner come together in cases of need, which they may stand in of one another.

The *other* is, that it may often happen, even among Animals of the same kind, that the Brain of the one is mov'd by the Voice or Cry of the other after such a manner, that it shall be more beneficial for that creature, whose Brain hath

82

hath been mov'd by that cry, to have
the spirits flow into other Muscles, than
those which serve to make a like voice.
For example, if a *Cock* makes that noise
he useth to make, when he meets with
a grain of corn, it may be, that that
noise striking the ears of the Hens, will
shake their Brain in such a manner, as
shall make them run to the place where
that grain is, without forming a voice
like that which made them come thither : As also it may happen, that one
Animal cries so, on the occasion of a
dangerous object, as that it maketh all
the other of the same *species* run away,
without forming any cry like it. But
as often as a Brute is not pressed by such
necessities, which do alwayes strongliest
determine the course of the spirit in its
Body, when its ear is struck by a Cry ;
that communication betwixt the Ears
and the *Larinx* maketh, that from the
same place, where the Nerves of the
Ear have made a motion in its Brain,
the spirits do necessarily flow into the
Muscles of the *Larinx*, which disposing
it in such a way, as is suitable to the impression

preſſion of the Brain do make the Animal form a cry altogether like it.

Thence it comes, that *Birds* excite one another to ſing: And in ſhort, this commerce between the Nerves of the Ear, and thoſe of the parts ſerving for the voice, is in *general* ſo much the cauſe of the noiſe, which moſt Brutes make, that (provided they are not in any urgent need) when their ears are excited by ſome noiſe, the impreſſion it makes in their Brain, cauſes the ſpirits, that are not diverted another way, take their courſe to the *Larinx* to diſpoſe it to make a like noiſe. And as the noiſe which hath ſhaken their Brain, cannot alwayes be imitated by the voices, which they are capable to make according to the natural conformation of their Throat, they often return ſuch as are very differing. Hence it is, that *Muſical* Inſtruments excite Birds to ſing, yet their ſongs are ſo different from all that is play'd on ſuch Inſtruments. But to ſhew, that that proceeds only from the little conformity there is between thoſe Inſtruments and the diſpoſition
of

of the Throat of the Bird, which hinders the imitation, we find that as often as there is a proportion between their throat, and the voices that strike their Ears, they fail not to form at length such as are like them.

Thus *Linets* learn in time the note of *Nightingales*, the songs of other Birds, and what ever is play'd on Instruments; and they learn even, as *Parrets*, to pronounce some of *our* words, because they have the *Tongue* and *Beak* disposed to articulate them. If they be long in learning the songs of other Birds, or our words, 'tis because the Nerves, which communicate from their ears to the muscles of their Throat, Tongue, and Beak, cannot be so soon adjusted to those new ways of voices, as to cause their formation presently; but it appears at last, that from the time that those parts are capable to form those voices, they do actually utter them.

And we ought above all things to observe, that the change which happens in them when they learn, is, that their Brain being divers times struck in the

same

fame place by the fame Songs, or the fame Words, the impreffion thereof remains fo ftrong in that place, that the fpirits which thence iffue to flow into the mufcles of their Throat, Tongue and Beak, do at laft difpofe them to repeat thofe fongs or words.

It is likewife to be well obferv'd, that they never return the fongs and words they have learnt, but when they are in no fuch need, which diverts their fpirits another way; and if in thofe neceffities they form a cry or voice, 'tis ever the cry or voice of their kind; fo that they form not ftrange fongs, nor utter human words, but when they want nothing, and when the fpirits, abounding or much heated, run, without any diverfion to their courfe, from the place of the brain, which thofe fongs or words have moft agitated, to the parts that ferve for the voice; except great care have been taken to give them none of the food they needed, but at the time when fome body did fing or fpeak near them: for then the prefence of the food does not fail to excite
them

them to repeat the same songs or words.

And to understand this well, we must conceive, that Brutes learn their cry from others of their kind, and that ordinarily the food is the cause of it. For their young ones, having at the same time their *Ears* struck by the cries, always made by their Dams at the presence of some food, which they have not yet the possession of, and their *Eyes* also struck by that food it self; it must come to pass, that the place of their brain which always receives those two agitations at once, gets thence in time such an impression made in it, that the spirits taking their course from that place to the throat and the muscles serving for the voice, must needs dispose them after such a manner, as answering to the impression of the brain, causeth those young ones to make a cry like that of their Dam.

But when they are brought up by men, and when *Linets*, for example, are bred in a Cage, and that in stead of the cry of their Dam, it happens, that

in

in the presence of the food, certain
strange songs or humane words strike
their ears; 'tis no wonder if those words
or songs (making impression in the
same place of the brain, whence that
food should have made the spirits to
flow into the muscles of the throat and
beak, to cause them to make the noise,
which birds make at the presence of a
food they hold not yet,) are cause that
the spirits being otherwise directed,
do also otherwise dispose the muscles
of the throat, tongue and beak, of
those young Birds, and make them sing
songs and utter words instead of the
cry, which they would have form'd,
if their Dam had bred them : This must
needs so happen; and even those songs
or words may then be call'd their natural cry or song, because having always accompany'd an action, that hath
made so deep an Impression on their
brain, it cannot be, that that action
should move their brain, and the spirits
should not also flow presently to the
muscles, which serve for that song or
those words.   And likewise, if they
have

have been put in a certain condition,
or in a certain place to make them learn
the better, they will sooner repeat what
they have been taught, if they be put a-
gain in the same condition and place,
than in any other.

'Tis easie also to understand, why it
hath sometimes happn'd, that a great
noise, as that of a *Trumpet*, having at
one blow shaken altogether the ear of
a Bird, hath made so strong an Impression in his brain, that having struck out
all the others, the spirits have no more
diffused themselves towards his throat,
than in such a manner, as might dispose
the muscles of the *Larinx* to return
sounds altogether like that of a Trumpet : And we must not wonder, if the
passages, through which those spirits
flow to the throat, being more difficult
to be moved, than the brain to be shaken, the Bird remains sometimes in a
kind of silence for many days, before he
renders that sound, nor also, if that
silence be perpetual, when the parts,
which serve for the voice, are not capable to form a like one to the sound,
which

which hath so strongly mov'd the Brain.

In short, there is no intelligent man, who after this discourse sees not, why an Animal being born *deaf*, must needs be *dumb*.

From all which it results with sufficient evidence to a considering Man, *first*, That 'tis the Lungs and the structure of the Wind-pipe, the mouth, the palat, the teeth, and the muscles of all those parts, which by receiving and repelling, or in diversly modifying the Air, is the cause, enabling us to form Voices, and to articulate them.

Secondly, That 'tis by reason of the communication, which is between the brains and the other parts of the body of every Animal, that it is diversly agitated by those Voices.

Thirdly, That in every Animal, capable to form Voices, there is such a commerce from the ear to the brain, and from the brain to all the parts serving for the voice, that the same voice which shakes the brain by the intervention of the ear, disposeth it also to diffuse the spirits into the muscles of those parts ;

90

parts; which spirits putting them into a posture answerable to the manner in which that voice did strike the brain, make them form a voice altogether like it, if some pressing necessity of the Animal diverts not the course of the spirits to another place.

Which being once well understood, it will be easie to know a thousand things, which commonly enough are not known touching the different effects of the cry and noise of Animals; which I mean not to explain more particularly, because that all those, who have attention enough to conceive the few principles, which I have laid down, will from thence draw all what is necessary to explain it, and because those that are not capable of such an attention, would not conceive what I could say of it even in a more particular discourse.

I shall only stay to consider here, that according to these Principles, Brutes need no Soul to cry, or to be moved by cries. For if they be toucht in any place, or their nerves struck with force enough to cause a great shake in
their

their Brain, 'tis sufficiently easie to conceive, that that action agitating the spirits, these must flow much more swiftly
into the muscles, and by this means the
swiftness of those that run incessantly
to the heart, augmenting, must render
the pulses thereof more precipitate;
which maketh it propel so great a plenty of bloud into the Artery of the Lungs,
that this Artery being more distended
than ordinarily, presseth the Wind-
pipe, and maketh the air to be driven
out of the Lungs with an impetuosity
answerable to that, whereby the bloud
enter'd there.

The second effect of this quick agitation of the spirits is, that at the same
time they flow to the heart, some of
them diffuse themselves also to all the
other muscles that are in a continual a-
ction, as those of the breast; because,
whereas the passages, through which the
spirits are conveyed in those sorts of
muscles, are alwayes open by reason of
the necessity of their continual action,
the spirits cannot receive a new motion
without presently communicating it to
those

those Muscles : which causeth those of
the Diaphragme and Breast press the
Breast in such a manner, as makes the
air issue out with unusual force ; and
seeing the muscles of the *Larinx* are
also strongly agitated , the air thence
getting out is beaten in a manner,
which holds somewhat of that agitation.

Thus it may be conceived from the
sole disposition of the Body, why a
Brute cries : And to know how it may
be *moved* by cries without having a Soul,
you need but remember the communion there is between the brain, the parts
serving for the voice, and all the parts
of the body. For, if according to the
difference of cries, the brains are diversly moved, and if following that diversity of the shakings of the brain, the
body is diversly carried, we need go no
further than their bodies, for a cause,
why Brutes of one and the same kind
are mov'd to come to one another by
the cryes they make, and why their
cryes often drive away those of *another*
kind. If we consider only that they
have

93

have a body so mechanically disposed, that the sole structure of it may be the cause that 'tis carried *to* such Objects, as may be good for them, and *from* such as may hurt them; me thinks, that how wonderful soever their motions may seem to us, we cannot rationally impute them, and particularly their cryes, but to the construction of their bodies; since, if we heed it well, we shall find in our selves, that the cries are not made but by the body alone.   For indeed, if we cry, 'tis not because we have a Soul, but because we have Lungs and other parts, which can receive and force out the air with certain modifications.

Likewise, if the Nerves of our Ears be mov'd by a voice, that is, by an air, which other bodies have agitated so, as that our brain shaken thereby, diffuseth spirits into the muscles of all the parts, whose motion can form a voice like that which mov'd it, that is, repell the air in a manner answerable to that which hath shaken it, it is upon no other account but that of our having a Body.

Lastly,

Laſtly, if our brain, when 'tis ſhaken by a noiſe or voice, ſends the ſpirits rather into the muſcles, that ſerve to carry our body near *to* or far *from* thoſe which cauſ'd that Noiſe, than into the muſcles of the *Larinx* or of the other parts, ſerving to form a like voice, it is becauſe we have a Body. So that, if there be nothing found in Brutes but the like effects, we cannot rationally ſay, that they have ought elſe but Body.

But as for Us, we muſt avow (whatever we adſcribe to our bodies in what regards the cauſes and effects of the voice) there is alwayes ſomewhat accompanying them, which cannot be from the *Soul.* For as 'tis true (to ſpeak in *general*) that it would be ſufficient to have motions, for which our body is fit, and to receive the effects which are wrought upon it by the various objects, that agitate the brain thereof, to conſerve our body, for as much as the proportion and relation God hath put 'twixt it and the other bodies of the World, gives it, without our thinking

B on't,

on't, all what can maintain it in a condition sutable to its nature : So 'tis true' also to say, that all *that* would be acted in us, and yet we *perceive* nothing of it, if we had nothing but the Body. But now, reflecting on what happens to us, when some noise strikes the nerves of our ear, we shall plainly find, that besides that shaking of the nerves of the Ear, which continuing to the very internal parts of the brain, doth there agitate the spirits, and makes them flow into the muscles, serving to move our whole body near *to* or far *from* that noise, there is always conjoyn'd a *Perception* to every shake of our ear, or of the other parts of our body : And at times we even find in us a *will* altogether contrary to the motions which that noise excites in our body. And although sometimes the impetuousness of those motions be such, that we can hardly stop them in their carriere ; yet 'tis manifest, that that contrariety would not be found in us, if what renders us capable to *will*, were not differing and altogether distinct from what makes us capable to *move*.   But

96

But of thofe two things which we find in our felves, befides *Motion*, I mean, the *Perception*, which we have, when-ever the nerves of our ear are fhaken; and the *Will*, which we have by confequent, *to confent* to the motion, to which our whole body is excited, or *to reſtrain* it; me thinks the latter is fo' evidently diſtinct from our body, that none but very inconfiderate perfons can be withont obferving and knowing the diſtinction.

As to the *Perception*, we have on the occafion of the fhaking, which the voice caufeth in the nerves of the ear, though it be fomewhat difficult to be diſtinguiſht from that fhaking, becaufe it always accompanies it; yet 'tis eafie to him, that is a little accuſtom'd to judge of the effects by their caufes, to find, that the fhaking, being a motion, cannot appertain but to our Body, and that the *Perception* being a Thought, cannot belong but to our Soul: And as we have found by other reflections, that the Union of our Soul and Body only conſiſts in this, that certain Thoughts

E 2   are

are so united to certain motions, that the one are never excited without the others be so too at the same time; we ought not to wonder any more to find, that the nerves of our ear shall never be shaken, but we shall presently feel in our Soul a *Sensation*, or, if you will, a *Perception* answerable to the manner the nerves are shaken in; nor ought we to believe, that that *agitation* and that *perception* are one and the same thing, although they always accompany one another.

We are therefore to consider two things in that we call *Sound*; one is the manner, in which the *Air*, striking the nerve of our ear, shakes our brain; and the other is the *Sensation* of our Soul on the occasion of that agitation of the brain. The *former* belongs necessarily to the Body, because 'tis nothing but a Motion; and the *latter* belongs necessarily to the Soul, because 'tis a *Perception*.

So likewise in *Speech* there are two things, *viz.* the Formation of the voice, which cannot come but from the Body,
according

according to what we have already dif-
courf'd; and the fignification joyn'd
with it, which cannot be but from the
Soul. So that *Speech* is nothing elfe
but a voice, by which we fignifie what
we think. 'Tis true, you may alfo (as
hath been already obferv'd above) joyn
your thoughts to other figns befides the
Voice, as to the characters of *Writing*,
or to certain *Geftures*, and that indeed
all thofe ways of expreffing our felves
are nothing but ways of *fpeaking* (to
take the word in a general and large
fenfe :) But then, becaufe the *Voice* is
the moft eafie figne, the word *Speech*
hath been appropriated to it, leaving to
Characters the word of *Writing*, and to
other ways of expreffing our felves the
word *Signe*, which is that of the *Genus*,
common to all thofe three *Species's*.

It may be I have already faid enough
of each of them, to make them to be
fufficiently diftinguifh't; but poffibly
alfo, fince I have not examin'd them
but on the fcore of what they have
common among themfelves, it may not
be ufelefs or tedious, to fpeak of them
apart,

apart, that it may appear wherein they differ one from another.

And to begin with that kind, to which hath been left the name of the *Genus,* I mean, the *Signes,* we muſt, to comprehend in a few words what may be known of it, take notice, that ſome of them are *natural,* others, that may be called *ordinary* or common, and others, that may be term'd *particular.*

The *natural* ones are thoſe, by which, becauſe of the neceſſary communion, which is between the paſſions of the ſoul, and the motions of the body, we know from without the inward different ſtates of the Soul. I have ſaid above, that theſe motions are the ſame in all men. But yet we are to remember, that ſince we may purpoſely conſtrain them, or excite them at pleaſure, we are not to truſt them too much, nor believe that they ſignifie always what they ſhould ſignifie.

The ſignes, which I call *ordinary,* are thoſe by which moſt men are wont to declare certain things, and thoſe are meerly of *inſtitution* : Some are more *univerſal,*

universal, others less. E. g. When we will, without a voice, say that we *consent*, we give a signe with the head, quite differing from that which we make to shew, we *consent not* : so we make certain signes with the hand to drive one away. And these kinds of signes are *general* enough; but those, by which we declare our respect to one another, though commonly they be the same in a whole Country, yet they are very different in another.

The signes I call *particular*, are those in which a whole Nation or a whole Commonalty agrees not, but which are instituted 'twixt two persons or a few more, to signifie certain things, which they would not have others to take notice of.

As for *Writing*, there is none that's *Natural*, and 'tis by *Art* only, that men have found out the secret of it. As they saw, that they could make *Gestures* and *Voices* to signifie what-ever they had a mind to, so they thought, that giving significations to *Characters*, which the hand might form, those

E 4   would

would be signes, which remaining for
a long time after us, would make our
thoughts known not only to those that
should be far off, but also to them that
should be born a great while after
them.

And this hath been done divers
ways. At first were used such characters,
whereof each signified *a Thing*; but
this way was troublesome, forasmuch as
men were to learn too many Characters, and to remember too many significations; besides that by that means
there could only be signified *Things*, but
Actions not conveniently.

Afterwards, as it was observ'd, that
all the diversities of Speech proceeded only from the different ways of forming Voices, or articulating them, and
that *Five voices* only, differently articulated, or diversly assembled, did form
all the words; it was thought fit, to
give a *Character* to each of those Voices: next there were instituted Characters to mark their *Articulations*; and
the assembling of those different characters made *syllables*, which being
joyn'd

102

joyn'd together did compose entire words : so that disposing those Chara-cters in an order like that we form the voices in, or the articulations which they represent, we remember the words, and those words make us remember the things they signifie. Thus we see, that *Writing* is a way of *speaking* to the E*yes*, which 'tis true demands more time to express, but then it lasts also much longer.

It hath likewise this other defect, that *few* persons can see at the same time the Thoughts of him that useth it; but since *that* is made up by this admirable advantage, of being able to signifie the thoughts of the *Writer*, notwithstanding the distance of places and times; it hath alwaies seem'd so great a convenience, that in seeking to supply what is wanted, men have at last found the *Art* of *Printing*, that is, of making Characters of mettal or wood, which being once ranged, and charged with ink or colour, can mark all the leaves, needfull to gratifie many to read at the same time and in divers places the same thing.   E 5   I

I do not discourse here, that there are wayes of writing, that are *ordinary*, and others, called *Cifers*, which are peculiar to certain people : Neither do I recite the way of expressing *Numbers* upon paper by characters that bear most commonly the name of *Cifers*; nor that of expressing *Sounds* by other characters called *Notes* : For all that is sufficiently understood of it self.

As to the way of expressing ones-self by the Voice, to which principally hath been given the name of *Speech*, we may say, that there are Voices *natural*; as those that are put forth in Grief, in Joy, and in the other passions. But (as I have already said of *Signes natural*, we must not always trust those voices, and they be often strained, or used to make others believe, that we resent what indeed we resent not.

There are other Voices, which men make use of to express to one another their thoughts : Some are more universally receiv'd , as those are which compose the Language of a whole People; others are more particular, used
by

by perfons, that agree amongft themfelves of words altogether new to fig-
nify their thoughts.

I have already taken notice, how we
begin to fpeak when we are little Children; how one may learn a new Language; and if there be any thing left to
be faid on this fubject, it will be to confider in this place, how he that learns
a new Language may turn it into a
habit.

For that, we are to obferve, that we
joyn from the time of the firft Language we learn, the *Idea* (or image) of
a thing to the *found* of a word; which
is entirely upon the fcore of the Soul.
For the fenfation, call'd *Sound*, and the
Image of the thing, made to be fignified
thereby, are all from the *Soul*, as we
have already made out. From the *Body's* part there is a motion of the fpirits
and brain, which every voice excites,
and an Impreffion, which every thing
leaves there : But that *motion* is alwaies
joyned to that *Impreffion*, as the *Perception* of every found is always joyned in
the Soul with the particular image of
this

105

this or that thing; so that when we will expresse the *Idea* of that thing, we conceive at the same time the *sound* of the voice, which signifies it : then, on the occasion of that *Idea*, and of the *Will* which the Soul hath, that the brain should duly dispose it self to diffuse the spirits into the parts, which are to form it; it comes to pass, that it is shaken at the place where the impression of that thing did remain, from whence the spirits flow into the muscles of the parts, which serve for the voice, to dispose them to form that which signifies what we have a mind to say : And as we have learned to joyn all those things from our Birth, that conjunction follows so close the will we have to speak, that we imagine that what is so readily done, must needs be much more simple ; and since we see not any Engin much composed, but it performs its effects with much difficulty, we can scarce believe, seeing the facility there is in *speaking*, that there should need so many parts to be acted for that purpose : But we must accustom our selves by admiring

the

the structure of our Body, to consider that 'tis made by an incomparable Workman, who is inimitable. Besides, if we are convinced, that the Union of the Body and Soul proceeds only from the perfect correspondence, which God hath establisht between the different changes of the brain, and the different thoughts of the Soul; we ought not to wonder, that the one acts so easily upon the other, and that their actions do always accompany one another so well, as long as God Almighty preserves their Union.

But in regard that this is one of the most important verities, that can fall under consideration, it will not be amiss, for the opening of all the difficulties thereof, to observe, that there are *three* kinds of Correspondencies between the Soul and the Body.

The *first* is *natural;* and that is that necessary correspondence, by which certain sensations rise always in the Soul, when certain motions are excited in the brain ; as motions are excited in the Body, when the Soul hath a will to it.

And

And this correspondence cannot abfolutely ceafe but with our life, and that
which wholly changes it; caufeth
death.

Befides this, there is a *fecond* Correfpondence 'twixt the *Idea's* the Soul
hath of things, and the Impreffions
which thofe things leave in the brain.
This correfpondence, no more than the
firft, cannot change altogether; and
whilft the Soul is united to the Body, fhe
never las the *idea* of things corporeal,
but their impreffion is in the brain.

But there is a *third* correfpondence
between the *Name* of every thing and
its *Idea,* which being only by *Inftitution;*
may be chang'd : but yet, in regard the
found of the firft name, men give to a
thing, is a fenfation, which the Soul
ftrictly joyns to the *Idea* of that thing;
and fince alfo the *impreffion* of that name
is found joyn'd to that of the thing in
the brain, we find it a trouble to fever
them : Whence it is, that when we begin to learn a Language, we commonly
explain by the *firft* word, by which we
nam'd a thing, the new word, by which
we

we intend to underſtand it in the
tongue, we are learning.

And there are even ſuch, whoſe brain
is ſo diſpoſed, that when they learn a
new Language, they always joyn to the
words of that, which they already know,
the words of the ſecond, to repreſent to
themſelves what they ſignifie.

Others, that have another diſpoſition
of the brain, do ſo eaſily joyn the ſound
of a new word in it ſelf to the *Idea* of
the thing, that that *Idea* is equally re-
preſented to them by the two words,
and they not obliged to think on the
one to underſtand the other.

Thus one may ſo well joyn one and
the ſame thought to many ſignes, and
to words of different Languages, that
one may with an equal facility uſe both
to expreſs it : But with a very little conſideration we may eaſily judge, *by* the
pains we find in the beginning, to joyn
the words of a new Tongue to the I-
mage of every thing ; *by* the neceſſity
we are in, to joyn the image of a new
word to that of an old, which made it
to be underſtood ; and even *by* the pains
we

we experience in pronouncing those
we learn, that *Speech* indeed depends
upon the relation and correspondency
of many things, and that, if afterwards
it becomes easie, 'tis only from the excellent composition of the brain, and the
admirable commerce between its motions and our thoughts.

For the rest, me thinks, if the Soul is
oblig'd, whilst she is united to the Body,
to joyn her thoughts to words, which
cannot be heard nor form'd without
the organs of the tongue and the ear;
She might, if that union ceased, much
more easily discover to every other *Spirit* what she did think. And truly if it
be a pain to him that examins it, to conceive, How the thought of a man that
speaks is joyn'd to the motion of his
brain, and the motions of his brain to
those of the parts serving for the Voice;
if it be difficult to comprehend, How
that Voice, which is nothing but Air
agitated, strikes the ear, and is able by
moving the brain to excite in his soul,
that hears the sound of the words,
the *Idea* of the things signifi'd by them;
if

if that, I say, is so hard to conceive, because we know, there is so strange a difference between the nature of the Spirit and that of the Body, we cannot but
easily comprehend, that if two Spirits
were not united to Bodies, they would
find less difficulty to discover to one a-
nother their thoughts, in regard there is
naturally much more proportion between the thoughts of two like Spirits,
than between the thoughts and the motions of two Bodies ; and upon the least
reflexion made on the facility and
clearness, with which one man conceives
the thoughts of another by *Speech*, we
shall avow, that a Soul might incompa-
rably more clearly and more easily conceive the thoughts of another Spirit, if
both of them depended not from the
organs of the Body. For a spirit sure
should more easily apprehend a thought
which is a thing spiritual, than the signe
of that thought, signes being things
Corporeal.

Thus I esteem, that 'tis much more
natural for spirits to manifest or to
communicate to one another their
thoughts

thoughts in themselves, and without a-
ny signes, than to speak to one another,
that is, to communicate their thoughts
by signes, that are of a nature so different from that of Thoughts : The pains
also which every one finds in conversation, and on all occasions where men
impart their thoughts by signes or
speech, is not to comprehend what a-
nother thinketh, but to extricate his
Thought from the signes or words,
which often agree not with it.

'Tis also the ignorance of the signes
and words, that is the cause, why men,
bred in different Countries, are a long
while together without being able to
understand one another : But as soon as
acquaintance hath afforded them all
what's requisite, readily to unfold what
every sign or word means, they find no
more trouble to conceive their thoughts,
of how different Nations soever they
be.   Which evidently shews, that men
understand one another naturally ; that
the thought of one is alwayes clear to
another, as soon as he can perceive it ;
and that, if there be men, who conceive
better

better than others what is said, that facility of understanding comes from the
structure of their brain, which being so
disposed, as that the impressions, I have
spoken of, are there more easily received, better ranged, and more distinctly
marked, makes the thoughts, answering
thereto, to be also more easie, more
consequent and more clear; whereas
those who want that good conformation
and disposition of the brain, must needs
be slower in conceiving, by reason of
that necessary correspondence and relation between the motions of the Brain
and the thoughts of the Soul, whilst she
remains united to the Body : But who
seeth not, that that entanglement would
cease, if the Soul were separated from
the Body?

'Tis also from the Fabrique of the
brain and the other parts serving for the
Voice, that the facility or difficulty of
the expression comes, and the pain,
that some have to speak, proceeds only
from hence, that the parts of their
brain, which answer to the thoughts of
the soul, or those that serve for the
Voice,

113

Voice, are ill dispos'd; but not from their Thoughts, which alwaies explain themselves clearly by themselves, and would never be obscure, if they were sever'd from the signes, or the Voices, employ'd to make them to be understood, and often not agreeing with them.

In short, that indispensable necessity, men are in, during life, to express themselves by words, is the cause that those, who naturally have their Brain better dispos'd in what may serve for the operations of the Soul; who have more vivid impressions of every thing; who know to range them better, and who are accustomed to express them in the most proper words; are alwayes those, that speak with most ease, the greatest agreeableness, and the best success: insomuch that if one will search well after the physical causes of *Eloquence*, they will be all found in that happy disposition of the Brain.

We know, that the *first* part of an excellent *Orator* is, to be able, easily to discern among all the things, that offer them-

themfelves to his Mind upon the fubject he is to treat of, what his Auditors are to know thereof; to the end that he may precifely tell them nothing but that; and 'tis evident, that unlefs he have a Brain difpos'd to keep the impreffions of every of thofe particulars very diftinct, he cannot make that due difcernment of them.

The *fecond* confifts in the well ranging of all what is able to make the things, he defigns to exprefs, to be underftood; fo as what is the moft fimple, the moft clear, and the firft in the order of nature, may ferve for a Light to clear up what follows, which of itfelf might be more obfcure : And that cannot be, when the parts of the Brain are ill difpos'd, or the courfe of the Spirits ill regulated; for then the impreffions of the things confounding themfelves, often prefent to the mind at firft, what ought not to be propos'd but at laft; or elfe they are ftirr'd with fo much precipitation, that the mind can neither reflect upon the order of every one, nor put it in its due place.

The

. The *third* is, to know well, and to find eafily the word, by which each thing is properly fignified in the Language, he ufeth; and that depends from the *Memory*, which cannot be fo faithful as it ought to be, unlefs the parts of the Brain be fo well ordered and in fuch a temper, as keeps the impreffions from confounding themfelves, and the *idea's* of one word from prefenting themfelves, when he feeks for another.

Thefe are the *three* things, that are abfolutely neceffary in the defign of *Inftructing*, which is only the *firft* part of *Eloquence* and thefe three things require a Brain of parts well order'd and ftay'd and a Courfe of Spirits very well regulated; which, if there were no more required, is very difficult to find.

But then, when we come to confider, that for the *other* part of Eloquence, which tends to *move*, we muft know the *Paffions* of the Auditors, and their fprings, in order to ftrengthen or to change them, according as fhall be requifite for the end aimed at; and that

The

116

the greatest secret, well to express a
Passion to excite the same in others, is
to feel it in our selves: we are obliged
to confess, that for the good success
therein, it seems that the parts of the
Brain cannot be agitated enough, nor
the Course of the Spirits be too impe-
tuous.

'Tis true, if we did speak to people,
that were onely subject to *Errour*, and
not to *Passions*, it would suffice to speak
the things in order, to explain them
clearly, and to prove them in order to
persuade the Auditors of them; and for
that purpose it would be sufficient, to
have the parts of the Brain well ordered, and a temper not to be easily
mov'd.

But commonly we speak to persons,
who besides *Errours* are so subject to
Passions, that they are not perswaded,
except you be *equally* furnisht with
what is requisite to *instruct*; and to
move ; and these two things depend
from two dispositions so opposite, that
'tis hard to finde men furnish'd with
Brains so temper'd and adjusted, as to
afford

afford both those perfections together.

We find also, that generally all those that are fit to *instruct* have a coolness, which makes them languid when they will *move*; and on the other hand, that those who are very apt to *move*, have a fire in them, which maketh that the Auditors cannot conceive, but with difficulty, what they say to *instruct*; Whereunto the Example which *Cicero* in one of his Discourses relates of two Orators, agrees admirably well. He saith, that one of them was furnisht with a great clearness of mind, but was of a cold temper; and seeing that he had twice try'd to get some accused persons quitted, without being able to make the judges resolve for it, though he had perfectly instructed them; he besought the *other*, whose *genius* was altogether different, to speak on their behalf; which succeeded wonderfully well: And *Cicero* observeth, that that vehement *Orator*, seing there remained no more for him but to *move* the Judges already *instructed*, composed himself some hours before he went to the Audience

dience, to speak of that matter in a private room with so much heat, that he was already in a sweat, when he came before the Judges, whom he constrain'd, by the vehemency of his action, to grant him what the first could not obtain of them by the strength of his reasons.

As often as I think on this case, I cannot but admire the advantages, which the *Relator* of it had in *both* the parts of Eloquence; and though I look upon him as the Pattern, which all those that mean to prosper in this Art, ought to propose to themselves, I avow, that he appears to me in-imitable. But he may serve as an Example to shew, that one and the same person may render himself capable to *move* and to *instruct*. I say, *render himself* capable; for I think not, that one may be *born* fit for both these things, if we consider only, what we naturally find in every one; and I think that of the two Talents, which serve to make a man perfectly eloquent, there is one that may be supply'd by study, when the other is in our nature: but this is not reciprocal.   F   And

And the better to examine this difficulty, we are to observe, that those who have a lively conception, have commonly the Passions violent, because they have all the parts of the brain very subtile and exceeding moveable; but ordinarily they have but little memory, and if they find things easily, they remember them difficultly. On the contrary, those that have the parts of the brain grosser and more fixt, conceive things less and less easily; on the other hand, their passions are not so prompt; but for a recompence, they retain longer both *things* and *passions*.

But 'tis easie to see, that this latter sort is capable to speak, when the business is only to *instruct*; but if the spirits of men are to be managed, and not to be informed of certain things till they have been inspired with certain passions those latter will never get their end. And if sometimes by virtue of observing other Orators, or by reading their Works, or by hearing them, they find out their Dexterities; they cannot imitate them but in *copying* them in subjects

jects altogether resembling those which such Orators have handled , without ever producing any thing matching the *Original* And even sometimes, for as much as the Memory is all their excellency and strength , they borrow the very words of those, whom they copy, and often they *name* their Authors to add some weight to the things, which they commonly deliver so little to purpose, and always so frigidly, that they would be intollerable, if they were not supported by some names in veneration among Great men.

Orators of this sort may exercise themselves long enough; they will never arrive higher than to be *Copists* of some one entire piece ; but they will never gain the dexterity to reunite many strokes of different Desseins, much less that of making new ones.

Whereas those that are of a contrary temper, having a lively and quick imagination, know easily the strength and weakness in a subject ; they soon discern what is to be declar'd, what to be hid : if they be obliged to say all, they

F 2   know

know how to prepoſſeſs the ſpirits before they propoſe what might be preju-
dicial to their Party, or diſpleaſe the
Auditor; and when they form the deſſein of their diſcourſe, if they imitate
other Orators, 'tis only as far as it a-
grees to their argument : And to ſpeak
truth, a Man of wit falls rather upon
the thoughts of the Great Men that
have been before him, becauſe *Reaſon*
ſuggeſts to him what hath been ſuggeſt-
ed to them, than becauſe he reads their
Works.

'Tis true, that that fecondity of the
mind that maketh him eaſily to conceive
and bring forth, may be the cauſe, that in
certain things he will be too much carried away, or diſpoſe them ill, or alſo
not be able to retain them; but theſe
defects are not without remedies.

The *firſt* may be ſupplied by a fre-
quent exerciſe of ſpeaking upon the
ſubjects, in which a man finds he is
wont to be moſt eaſily carried away,
and by accuſtoming himſelf not to paſs
certain bounds which he preſcribes to
himſelf, or maketh his friends preſcribe

to

to him; and 'tis not hard to give to one
self these reins, after a man once knows
his propenseness to be transported.

To remedy the *second* inconvenience,
a man must accustom himself to mar-
shall his thoughts, and to order them
well upon all the subjects he proposeth
to himself, of what nature soever; and
as the way of *declaring* them is very different from that of *conceiving* them, he
must, to accustom himself to speak well
what he knows, often ask himself, how
he would declare this or that matter,
if he should be obliged thereto; in
what manner he would handle the *same*
subject before a great multitude of people, or before a less Assembly; what
would be said of it, if spoken before
persons of power and honor, or before
his Equals; and to render this practise
more usefull, he is to examine when o-
thers have spoken in publick, wherein
'tis they have succeeded well, & wherein been deficient; and even to endeavor,
after having found the cause of their
failure, to make up the same discourse
better than they did; and to continue
F 3   these

thefe Exercifes until one's mind be accuftom'd well to digeft all forts of fubjects.

As to the *third* Inconvenience, which
is that of the Memory, feeing that that
cannot be defective, but in not repre-
fenting to us the *things*, or in not fur-
nifhing us with the *words*; there is a
remedy for the firft defect, by putting
the *things* in fo natural an order, that
the one muft needs make you remember the other by the connexion they
have together; and then, after a man
hath form'd the deffein, and order'd all
the parts of a difcourfe, he muft often
revolve and repeat it with himfelf, to be
accuftomed to it.

For the *Words*, we are not to fear
their eafie occurring to us for fpeech,
when the matters are prefent to our
Mind, if fo be we are accuftomed to
fpeak. And for that purpofe, a man muft
impofe upon himfelf the neceffity of
fpeaking upon all forts of fubjects, accuftom himfelf, by writing, to vary and
turn them every way, and alwayes to
chufe the moft difficult or the moft ab-
ftract

stract matters. For when by the force of searchng a man can find ways to make *those* things to be understood, he hath almost no difficulty to find words and expressions in all other subjects, that are more ordinary, and which the various necessity of Life render more common.

After we have thus examined, How much Eloquence depends from mens Temper, and how *that* may be corrected or perfected by Exercise; it will not be amiss to consider, That there is no greater Enemy to true Eloquence, than *Lying* : And as Eloquence is a means not only to expresse what we think, but also to oblige *others* to think as we do, it ought never to be employed but to manifest *Truth*, or to make it to be embrac'd and follow'd ; and he that employes it to excite in others unjust sentiments, or to make them believe things that are false, commits the most hainous of all treacheries. For tell me, I pray, if human society be not entertain'd but by *Speech*, is it not a violation of the most sacred right that is amongst men,

F 4 to

to employ, for the leading of them into error, or for perfuading them to e-
vil, fuch endowments as ought to ferve
only to make them know what's *true*
or *juft* ? If this were ferioufly thought
on, there would be much more fince-
rity ; efpecially when men fpeak in publick, where the leaft difguifes may draw
after them **very** dangerous confequen-
ces For the reft, me thinks, that to
make us accuftom our felves to
fpeak nothing but truth, 'tis a powerful
motive, often to reprefent to our felves
that we have not the facility to expreffe
our felves, but becaufe God Almighty,
to whom we owe our thoughts and the
motions of our tongue, is very willing
to excite the one, when we will make
known the other. Me thinks, 'tis in a
manner impoffible for one, that makes
often this reflexion, to lye. For, I pray,
if we be convinced, that God is not
fubject to error, nor to a lye, nor to
any iniquity, which alwayes follows it
fo clofe ; how can we employ Signs and
Voices, which are not form'd but by
his power to do that, which difpleafeth
                                    him

him moſt? I admire, that a Heathen came to know this truth ſo far, as to ſay, *That no man could be eloquent, except he were honeſt*; and that *we* ſhould have ſuch contrary ſentiments.

But not to mix here *Morality* farther than 'tis ſutable to a Diſcouſe of *Natural* Philoſophy, it will be to our purpoſe to examine in this place, whence it is, that not only an *Orator* ought to be a man of integrity, but alſo that he cannot be perfectly eloquent, unleſs he be ſo? And this is not hard to conceive : for, if it be agreed on, that to be perfectly eloquent, a man muſt know the Art to inſtruct his Auditors, and that of raiſing or allaying Paſſions, according, as it ſhall conduce to the end, that is propoſed; we muſt alſo agree in this, that an *Orator*, that ſpeaks the contrary to what he knows, will not ſo eaſily find words to expreſſe it, as if he ſpoke the truth ; and if to avoid miſtaking, he ſtudies what he is to ſay, it muſt be acknowleged, that his Diſcourſe, which will be but a piece of Memory, can never have that grace nor force, which is found in

F 5   that

that of a person, who having learnt to speak well, and speaking what he thinks, fears not, he should mistake.

Again, it must be granted, that if he, that is not an honest man, will excite in others the motions and passions, which really are not in himself, 'twill always go off coldly, to express passions studied; and if, to surmount the effect of that constraint, which appears when a man will refrain his own motions to fain others, he will blot out all the strokes and the little motions, by which his Countenance, Eyes, and Gesture would shew the contrary to what his Words do express, he must so exceedingly strain, that not only he loses the grace, without which a man cannot please nor persuade, but also renders himself odious, and is so far from exciting in others the motions which he hath not in himself, that he begets horror in all those, who perswade themselves, that he indeed feels the *violence* of the passions, wherewith he appears to be moved.

In a word, 'tis evident, that there is naturally such a relation between the Sentiments

timents of men, and the Signes and
Words used to express them, that one
and the same person can never tell a
Lye so gracefully as a Truth : And as a
man cannot be very eloquent, when he
constrains to *say* what he doth not
think, or to express what he feels not ;
'tis impossible to be very eloquent, unless one be very sincere and honest, seeing it belongs only to a man of integrity
to speak nakedly what he thinks ; his
motions are so just, that he needs not
to put on any constraint; besides, the
Truth, which accompanies all his words,
and that love of Justice, which animates
all his motions, give so much weight
and grace to his action, that 'tis in a
manner impossible to resist it ; and
which is the chief, we are easily carried
away by the motions of a man, whom
we believe to be Virtuous : and when
he, that speaks, hath the advantage of
exciting in others the same passions
which himself resents, as he is soon ma-
ster of their thoughts, so he soon renders their judgment favorable to what
he aims at. And since we see, that those,
whom

whom a like difposition of body maketh lyable to the like motions, have ordinarily the fame fentiments about the fame things, we may juftly believe, that the faireft means to gain others to the fame opinion with ours, is to raife motions in them altogether like ours. For indeed (which particular cannot be too often repeated) as long as our Souls remain united to our Bodies, all our motions will be fo confonant with our fentiments, that we fhall never be able to infpire the one but by the other.

This reflexion maketh me think, that as we can conceive Spirits not united to Bodies, if there be eloquence amongft them, *that* cannot be by the means of *Motions*, becaufe they are not capable of them: But fuppofing, that thofe Spirits are in that ftate of liberty, wherein they can determine themfelves to this or that thing, 'tis eafie to conceive, that if one of them, being more enlightned than others, hath a paffion for a thing, which a meer fpirit is capable to have a paffion for, (as for example, for his own glory) he may put his thoughts, which

he

he shall manifest to others upon that
subject; into an order which shall
appear so excellent, that it shall excite in some the same passion which
he resents; and on the other hand
(to keep to the same example) a
Spirit yet more illuminated and better
inclined than the former, may make
those, who might have fallen into that
error, to conceive, that, whereas that
Glory can appertain to none but the
Soverain Power, 'tis a folly for any one
to pretend to it, when he is not God.

It might after the same manner be
conceived, how meer spirits might inspire one another with divers sentiments
touching all such things for which they
were capable to have passions, supposing (as hath been said) that they
were in a state of chusing one of two.

But to draw from this notion no more
than may serve for my intent, it is to be
considered, that if for speaking a man
needs the motion of the parts that serve
for the voice, and if for hearing there
is need of the agitation of the parts, that
serve for Hearing; there needs nothing
betwen

between two Spirits, to communicate
their thoughts to one another, but to
will it : And since we find, that the
thought of one man is easily understood
by another, from the time that the first
hath spoken, that is, from the time that
by the motions, which serve to beat the
Air, he hath moved the Ear of him, to
whom he will have his thought known ;
'tis also easie to apprehend, that if two
Spirits, who depend not from the Body
in their operations, will discover to one
another their thoughts, they have nothing to do but to *will* it : There is, me
thinks, much less difficulty to conceiv the
one than the other (as I have already
observed :) For in *Speech* there are two
things, *viz.* the *Will* to communicate
one's thoughts, and the *Motions* by
which they are communicated ; but
those Motions have so little affinity, in
themselves, to the thoughts, that it
seems very strange, how a thought can
be so well united to a motion, as that
the one should be an occasion to know
the other ; whereas in the manifestati-
on, which two Spirits make to one another

other of their thoughts, there needs nothing but the *Will* to communicate them; and Spirits being of one and the same nature, 'tis evident that one *Thought* may much easier be the occasion of another thought, than *Motion.*

But next, what hath been said of the Communication of two *meer* Spirits, ought to be said of the commerce that may be betwixt a Spirit united to a Body, and one that is not. For certainly what incapacitates two men to communicate their thoughts to one another without motions, is, that they have Bodies, and that the one cannot be advertis'd by the other but by the motions occasion'd by the Body, to which the Soul is united: But supposing that one of the Spirits have no Body, it is capable to render it self present by its very thoughts to that which hath a Body, as it doth to that which is destitute of a Body; and reciprocally that Spirit, which is united to a Body, will be able, without the intervention of the Voice, to express its thoughts to every Spirit that is Body-less.   Mean

Mean time we are so accustom'd to judge of all things, by those we see, that since men make use of a voice, and very easily understand one another, we rashly judge, that it would be very difficult to two Spirits mutually to communicate their thoughts : And some judge it even impossible, that a Spirit, destitute of Body (for example, an *Angel)* should communicate with *Us.* But 'tis evident, that that proceeds only from the precipitation of our Spirit, who maketh no reflection on what befals him in the communication, he hath with the spirit of another Man. For if he did consider, that the beating of the Air, and the other things, which serve to make him understand the thoughts of the person that discourses with him, have nothing in them resembling those thoughts ; he would more wonder, that he understands him, than he wonders, when one will perswade him, that two *Angels* speak to one another, or that even one *Angel* can converse with *Us,* without the assistance of a voice.

I cannot in this place forbear to take
notice,

notice, how much the reflexion, we make on what passeth *within us*, is capable to make us judge aright of what is done, or at least may be done *elsewhere*. And the Example I draw from the manner, after which we converse with men, is so proper to make it to be conceived, what might pass betwixt Spirits destitute of such Bodies as we have, and even between those Spirits and Us, that, the thing being well examin'd, there will be found no other difference between those two sorts of Communications, but that that, which is between Man and Man, will prove the more difficult to conceive, in regard it is made by the means of *Motions*, which are quite different from *Thoughts*, whereas that, which we may have with meer Spirits, is less sensible, because 'tis perform'd without any of those motions, which render as 'twere sensible to us the thoughts of the men, whose voice striketh our *Ears*.

And this may be also the cause, why we are inform'd, that when Spirits would give any important advertise-

ments

ments to Men, they borrow'd Bodies,
and form'd Voices like those of Men.
But those Extraordinary things are not
to hinder us from conceiving, that naturally we can communicate with *meer*
Spirits more easily than with *Men.* So
that if Faith teaches us, there are Spirits
not united to Bodies, and that he, who
hath created them as he hath us, having
committed to them the care of condu-
cting us, they are always present to our
Spirit to direct it without constraining
it; there is nothing in that, which is a-
bove those things, we think we know
best. For in short, as we conceive, that
the communication between two Men
is made by *Speech,* that is, by a *Will* to
express what they think, and by the
motions answering to that will, we may
also, me thinks, conceive, that the converse of two Spirits may be made by the
sole Will of manifesting themselves to
one another; and that if a meer Spirit
communeth with a Man, though that
be in a way less sensible than is that of
ordinary Words, yet 'tis after a manner
intelligible, which may insensibly give
him

him the thoughts, he needs for his conduct; which in a word, is, to inspire him. Even so may we easily conceive, that God, who causeth our Spirits to move Bodies, can (if need be) give to an Angel the same power to make himself to be understood by speech.

Now, me things, I see, what is properly meant by the word *Inspiration*; and I believe, I am not deceived, when I say, that 'tis by that means only, that those thoughts may come into our mind, which have no affinity to any of those, that naturally are in our Soul, only because we have a Body.

Next, I see, that we know no more the Spirits of any of all those men, that speak to us, when they inspire us with their thoughts, than those *meer* Spirits, which I think capable to inspire us better thoughts. And as the new thoughts, which come into our mind by the conversation we have with men, are a sure testimony to any of us, that they have a Spirit like ours, we are to take the new thoughts coming in to us (without being able to find the cause of them in our

137

our selves, or impute it to the discourse
of men) for an assured testimony, that
there are yet other Spirits, that may inspire us with them.

I find also, that the custome of understanding the thoughts of other men
by gestures and the voice, maketh that
way to affect us more, than the things,
which are inspired us without it. But if
I heed it well, I see, that we do not
more know the Spirits of men that speak
to us, than the Spirits that inspire us.
A like Air, thrust out by the Lungs of
him, that discourses with us, striking
our ears, exciteth, upon the agitation of
the Brain, sounds in our Soul, and at
the same time the images or conceptions which we have joyned to those
sounds : But in truth, neither that propelled Air, nor any thing of what passeth into the Body from him that speaks
to us, is his thought ; and if we have a-
ny reason to believe him to have
thoughts, 'tis only because we feel, that
he excites new ones in us. But if all the
reason, we have to believe, there are
Spirits united to the Bodies of the men
that

that fpeak to us, is, that they give us often new thoughts, fuch as we had not,
or that they oblige us to alter thofe we
had ; can we doubt, when new thoughts
come into us, that are above our natural light, and contrary to the fentiments which the Body may excite in
us, can we, I fay, when no men infpire
us with them, doubt of their being infpired us by other Spirits ? I judge, we
cannot reafonably; and the cuftome,
we have to receive them by the means
of Speech, which is a fenfible way,
ought not to make us difadvow thofe,
that are infpired us by a way different
from that of the fenfes.

I know alfo, that if we be free to
hide our thoughts, whilft our Soul is u-
nited to a Body, we might have the
fame liberty, if it were feparated from
it ; and that in fome manner that free-
dome would yet be greater, in regard
that often when we fpeak to a perfon,
the fignes and the voices, by which we
exprefs our felves, may be perceived
or underftood by a Third, to whom we
would not difcover our thoughts;
where-

whereas a pure Spirit, who is not obliged to make use of those external signs, can manifest his thoughts to the Spirit he will inform, so as no other shall know of it.

In effect, in that state we now are in of discovering our thoughts, we do nothing else but to *will*; and although that *will* be joyned to motions, which fail not to be in certain parts of our body as soon as we need it for the signifying our thoughts; yet notwithstanding our souls are not the cause of those motions (according to what we shewed in our 4th Discourse *) and they do nothing else to express themselves but to *will*, so that as long as they are united to our Bodies, we cannot express the thoughts coming into our mind but by moving the Tongue, the Throat and the Mouth; this necessity is imposed on us by that union: But as soon as there should be no such necessity to borrow motions for expressing what we think, there would need no more to make other Spirits understand

* In his book entitl'd, *Le Discernement du Corps & de l'Ame.*

140

ftand it, but to *will* that they fhould
underftand ; and if we would have it
hid from them, there would need no
more than *not* to *will* that they fhould
know it.

I have elfewhere deliver'd the reafons, by which it appears, that all the
action of the Soul confifts in *willing*,
and I think I have fufficiently made it
out, that all what depends from Her,
is, to determine herfelf to one thing or
another, fo as I fhall not need here to
repeat any thing of what I have faid on
that fubject : But it will not be amifs to
take notice in this place, that although
God do not make us conceive, what is
the fubftance of our Spirits, nor how
they *will*, that is, how they determine
themfelves ; yet we know clearly, that
we have a Spirit, and that our Spirit hath
the power of determining it felf. But
now, as we are affured, that we fpeak
not our thoughts but when we pleafe,
we ought to believe, that if we were in
a ftate to need fignes and voices no
more, we might then by our *will* alone
difcover or hide our thoughts.

We

We are also to remember, that 'tis not more difficult to conceive, that *then* we should make our thoughts to be apprehended by other Spirits, than to conceive, that the spirit of another man should apprehend, in the present state, what we think, when we express it by voice or by signes.

For the rest, when I say, that Souls emancipated from the Body might hide or manifest their thoughts to one another; *that* is to be understood, if they had the same reason to hide their thoughts, they have now in the present state. But 'tis apparent, that, if they shall be happy, as they will have no thoughts but for the Glory of their Maker, so they will be glad that all the Spirits should know them; and if they for ever lose his grace, they will have only such thoughts, which being to serve to publish the effects of his justice, will be known to all the Spirits.

Lastly, we ought to remember, that according to what I have deliver'd of the Action of Souls and Bodies, in the *fifth Discourse* of the *first part*, we say, that

that one Soul acts upon another Soul, as often as one hath new thoughts upon an occasion given by the other; even as we say, that one Body acts upon another Body, as often as one Body receives some change upon occasion afforded by the other : And as I have shewn, that a Body never gives any motion to a Body, but only for as much as their meeting together is an occasion to the *Divine Power*, which moved one, to apply it self to the other ; We are also to conceive, that when one Soul will make known to another Soul what she thinketh, that happens forasmuch as Almighty God brings it to pass, that according to the will of the one, the other comes to know it : And even as the *Will* we have, that our Body be mov'd, does not make it move, but is only an occasion to the *First Power* to move it after such a manner as we desire it should be mov'd; so the *Will* also, which we have, that a Spirit should know what we think, is an occasion to that *Power* so to order things, that all may be disposed in such a way, as that

G   that

that Spirit may understand it.

Thence it necessarily results, that 'tis as impossible for our Souls to have new perceptions *without God*, as 'tis impossible for the Body to have new motions without Him. And 'tis evident besides, that our Souls, which depend from Him for their Being and for their Conservation, depend not at all from Him for the *Use of their Will*, whereof he leaves the determination altogether free. And I dare deliver it as a thing that will appear manifest to all men of good sense, who shall attentively consider it, that as the Body is a substance, to which *Extension* belongs naturally, so that it would, as to effects naturall, cease to be a Body, if it ceas'd to be extended; even so the Spirit is a substance, to which the power of determining it self doth so naturally appertain, that it would cease to be a Spirit, if it ceas'd to *will*; and God Almighty hath made it thus, that he might be loved by it. Which appears so evidently, that if he had not declared it by so many miraculous testimonies of his tenderness,

tenderneſs, which goes ſo far as to ask
of us our Heart, that is to ſay, our Love;
we ſhould be altogether perſwaded,
that He will be the object of our *will* in
this World, by this only conſideration,
that there is no object ſo great, but it
can embrace it.

As to the power of *knowing*, perhaps
he hath not given us that ſo great, at
leaſt not in this World. But 'tis certain,
that we have knowledge enough, as not
to fail, if we uſe well the light we have,
and the power we are endowed with,
of judging of nothing, but after we do
well know it. For, God gives us all the
light we need; we have *idea's* very diſtinct, to know the things of Nature as
much as 'tis uſefull to know them, ſince
we can, when we uſe prudence, diſcern
wherein every one is beneficial or hurt-
full to us: And although, according to
what I have already obſerv'd, he afford-
eth us not the advantage to know the
very ſubſtance of things, yet he ſo well
diſcovers to us, wherein they can hurt
or profit us, that to uſe it aright, we are
only to will it.   G 2   As

As for thofe things, which are *above Nature*, although they infinitely furpafs our knowledg,yet we have very diftinct notions of the Reafons, why we are not able to *conceive* them, and of the Reafons alfo, why we are to *believe* them. For if on the one hand in the doctrine of Faith there are things to be found, that are beyond our natural light; we have on the other, fuch evident fignes of the Obligation for us to fubmit our Spirit to his Authority, who propofeth them to us, and fo great convictions of our unablenefs to comprehend all what is; that we have caufe to take all, what comes to us from thence for infallible Truth; in a word, for Notions which we hold from *Grace*; and from which, as well as from thofe which we hold from *Nature*, we may deduce all the Conclufions that may ferve to regulate our Belief, and the Conduct of our Life, fo that we are guilty,when by inconfide-ration or obftinacy we deviate from thofe Rules.

But without infifting on the confide-
ration

ration of all the great Truths, that
might be collected from this whole Difcourfe, I think it will become me to
conclude, after I have confider'd all the
feveral wayes, whereby Thoughts may
be communicated, which is properly
what we call *Speaking*, and which I had
propofed to my felf to examine.

FINIS.

147

A
DISCOURSE
Written to a
LEARNED FRIER,
BY
M. *DES FOURNEILLIS*;
SHEWING,

That the S Y S T E M E of M. *D E S CARTES*, and particularly his Opinion concerning BRUTES, does contain nothing dangerous ; and that all he hath written of both, feems to have been taken out of the Firft Chapter of *G E N E S I S*.

To which is annexed the
SYSTEME GENERAL
Of the fame
CARTESIAN PHILOSOPHY.

By *Francis Bayle*, Dr. of Phyfick at *Tholofe*.

Englifhed out of *French*.

LONDON,
Printed , and are to be fold by *Moſes Pitt* at the *White Hart* in *Little Britain*, 1670.

149

A
DISCOURSE

Written to a Learned Frier, shewing that the Systeme of M. Des Cartes, and particularly his Opinion concerning Brutes, does contain nothing dangerous ; and that all he hath written of both, seems to have been taken out of the First Chapter of GENESIS.

My Reverend Father,

 Know very well, that *Moses* hath not written his *Genesis* with a design to explain to men the Secrets of Nature ; but I do also know, that being inspired by God, as he was,

A 2   he

151

he could say nothing about the production of the World, which is not true. And therefore I esteem, that to find the Principles of Natural Philosophy infallible, they are not to be sought but in that History which He hath given us of the Creation of the World; or at least, that we ought to esteem false whatever is said of Nature, when it cannot be reconciled with all the Circumstances of this History.

Do not wonder therefore that I so often refer you to *Genesis*, and that I lay so much weight upon the Principles of Monsieur *Des Cartes*. Most of his Tenets are so conform to what *Moses* hath said, that it seems, he became a Philosopher only by the Reading of this Prophet. But that you may the more easily apprehend how great an agreement there

there is between that Sacred
Writing and his Philofophy, I
intend to expound unto you the
firſt Chapter of *Geneſis* literally;
and you'l ſee, that in doing ſo, I
ſhall diſcourſe to you almoſt the
ſame things which I told you laſt,
when I explained to you the
Principles of M. *Des Cartes.*

The only difference you'l find
is, that M. *Des Cartes* writeth
things more particularly, and
with a deſign to make them
known what they are in themſelves; whereas *Moſes* writeth
like an Hiſtorian, who diſcour-
ſeth of Nature only ſo far as was
needful to make us admire the
power of the Author thereof.
Thus the one ſpeaketh only of
the principal things, and the o-
ther dives more into particulars;
and yet all theſe particulars are
clearly nothing elſe but a more

A 3　　　ample

ample explication, and a Sequel
of thofe main things which *Mofes* hath recited in fo concife, fo
bold, and fo true a manner.

I told you the other day, that
M. *Des Cartes* in the beginning of
his Principles ufeth much reafon-
ing to fhew, *That* there is a God :
That all what is, is only by him :
That he begun this great piece of
Workmanfhip, which we call
the World, by creating Bodies :
That from that time he moved
them, and that he ftill continues
to move them. I alfo told you,
that among fo many differences,
which the *Figures* may make between Bodies, M. *Des Cartes*
takes notice of three principal
ones; that he fhews, there is a
very great Number, of fuch as are
round like little Balls; others,
fubtil enough to fill the fpaces left
by thefe Balls between themselves;

felves; and others again, whofe
irregular Figures do fo entangle
them one with another, that they
may compofe the greater Maffes.

I added, that examining the
feveral changes, which the Matter or the Aggregate of all thefe
Bodies may have fuffered fucceſ-
fively, M. *Des Cartes* fheweth,
that there may have been formed
many Maffes of different big-
neffes, of a figure approaching to
that of the Earth; above which
he fheweth, that there was to
remain a number of particles,
fome like thofe which compofe
the *Water*, and others like thofe
which compofe the *Fire :* That
this Aggregate of Earth, Water,
and Air, was to be mixed, and
furrounded with an almoft infinite number of thofe little Bodies made in the form of *Globules*, and with thefe other fub-
A 4   tiler

tiler ones that were to fill up
their Intervalls. And that, lastly, M. *Des Cartes* repeats often,
that God entertains in a continual
motion this subtile matter, which
else could not be moved.

Now all this, if you mark it,
is nothing else, than to describe
Philosophically and exactly (for
the making out of the least circumstances of it) the same wonders which *Moses* hath described
Historically in these few Lines;
God created in the beginning Hea-
ven and Earth. Now the Earth
was void, and brought forth no-
thing, because it was covered with
deep waters; Darkness was upon
the face of this Abyss, and the
Lord moved a subtil matter upon
the Waters.

He that shall well examine
what

156

what the *Prophet* hath said, will
find that 'tis the same thing which
the *Philosopher* hath endeavoured
to explain.

The First Day.

IF we shall follow the one in
the progress of his Reason-
ings, and the other in the progress of his History; we may
judge, that it is of *Moses*, that
Des Cartes hath learned, that the
Light was made before the Sun ;
at least it will appear, that this
place of *Genesis* , which for so
many ages hath perplexed mens
spirits, is found happily cleared,
according to the Letter, by the
Principles of M. *Des Cartes.*

Moses

157

Moses having shewed that the Earth was infertile because of the Waters encompassing it, and the Celestial matter useless, because the motions of it were not regulated; he goes on to shew, that God, who does nothing in vain, began, for the ordering of all these things, with the Creation of *Light*: He expresseth himself magnificently, as he is wont to do; and maketh the Almighty speak on this occasion in such a manner, which is capable all alone to perswade, that it is the Lord himself that made him speak thus.

Behold his Expressions; *And God said, Let there be Light, and there was Light.* He adds, That God saw, his work was good; that he divided the Light from the Darkness; and that he gave the name of *Day* to the Light, and

and the name of *Night* to Darkneſs.

There is no man of good-ſenſe, who ſees not, that *Moſes*, having declared, that in the beginning God created Heaven & Earth,& that certain Bodies,ſubtil enough to be called Spirits, were carried to and fro, does ſignifie, that all the Bodies were already created; and that God did maintain from that time in the whole maſs of matter as much motion,as he conſerves in it now ; and that what he hath made in all the following ſix dayes, was only to put thoſe Bodies in order, and to regulate all their motions.

So that, if ſpeaking like an Hiſtorian, *Moſes* hath marked out the firſt day of this admirable Contrivance by the formation of Light, this ſignifies only to us, that God diſpoſed the Bodies

dies

dies, as they ought to be, to produce this wonderful effect; which
was sufficient for an Historian;
but the Philosopher was to make
it out, how these Bodies were to
be disposed for that purpose.

Wherefore chusing from among
all the Figures . those , which
might be most proper for the little Bodies which cause Light, and
seeing that those, which he had
described as *Globules*, being moved in a certain manner, would
be satisfactory to all that is known
of the Rayes which are made by
the Light ; M. *Des Cartes* hath
supposed, that there were formed divers *Vortexes* or *Whirl-pools*
of these little round Bodies, and
that many of them turning round
about one and the same Center,
a part of the matter, which fills
up their Intervalls, was gathered
towards the Center, whence it
did

did propel the *Globules* which surrounded it ; so that this pressure of the *Globules* made Light in all those places , where was found a sufficient conflux and heap of subtile matter.

But he adds, that as in this beginning there was not yet a great plenty of these more subtil parts in the Centers of the Whirlpools, the action, which pressed the *Globules*, did not reach far ; so that the places, which its effect could not reach to, remained in darkness, whilst the other were already enlightned : which agreeth admirably with the effect, which *Moses* ascribeth to the first Word of the Lord, which did separate the Light from the Darkness, from the time it began to form it : From thence also we may say, according to *Genesis*, that the Night was where the Darkness had

had remained; and the Day,
where the Light had begun.

You will obferve, that by the
Word *Light*, we are here to underftand nothing elfe but that,
which is the caufe, that the Bodies, called Luminous, excite in
us the fentiment,, which makes
us perceive them, and not the
fentiment it felf.

Men do often confound thefe
two things, and 'tis certainly from
thence that all the doubts proceed that are met with on this
Subject. But me thinks, that in
what *Mofes* hath written of Light,
'tis evident, that he would only
fpeak of what is found on the
part of the Bodies, and not of
the Effect which it produceth in
fuch Subjects as are capable to
have the fenfe of it ; fince it is
certain, according to *Mofes*, that
when that, which is called Light,
was

was created, there was yet none
of the other Creatures which are
efteemed capable to perceive
it.

I defire you to obferve by the
by another thing, which is ; That
this fentiment , which we have
from Luminous Bodies, is in fuch
a manner on the part of our Soul,
and hath fuch a neceffary refpect
to the motion of certain parts of
our Brain, that very often, without the excitation of the nerves
of our Eyes by any Luminous body, we have the fenfe of Light.
Thus in Dreams, the fortuitous
courfe of the Spirits moving
thofe parts of our Brain, the a-
gitation whereof is defigned to
excite in us that fentiment, maketh us clearly fee Objects that
are not prefent: And by the
fame reafon thofe, who marching
in a very obfcure place hurt their
head

head againſt the Wall, are ſub-
ject to ſee a thouſand Fires;
whence we are to conclude, that
thoſe motions of the Brain which
have nothing that reſembleth the
thoughts which ariſe in the Soul
on their occaſion, may be excited by other Bodies than thoſe
we call Luminous. But it was
very proper, not to give this
name but to Bodies, whoſe figure
and motion were ſo proportio-
nate to the fineneſs and tenderneſs of our Eyes, that their nerves
might be moved by them without pain, and without danger to
the other parts of our Body.
Wherein, me thinks, M. *Des
Cartes* hath ſucceeded admirably
well; it being not poſſible to aſ-
ſign to Luminous Bodies a fitter
Figure than that which he hath
given them, nor a motion more
convenient, than that which he
hath aſcribed to them.   The

The Second Day.

M*oses* relating what paſſed the Second Day, for the formation of the Firmament, expreſſeth himſelf in theſe terms; *God ſaid, let the Firmament be in the midſt of the Waters, and let it ſeparate the one from the other.* He adds, that the Firmament was preſently made, and the Waters were ſeparated from the Waters, ſo that there were ſome of them above and ſome under the Firmament, which he called *Heaven*.

To underſtand how the Waters were ſeparated one from the other by the formation of the Firmament, according to the ſentiment of M. *Des Cartes*, we ſhall

B   need

165

need only to relate what he
teacheth of the Waters and of
the Firmament.

Thofe who have read what he
hath written thereof, do know,
that after he had confidered all
the effects of Water, he conceived
that the particles, which compofe
it, muft be fmooth, long and
pliant ; and that by this fuppofi-
tion alone he hath rendred a reafon of all what is obferved in
Water, whether it be running,
or whether it enlarge it felf in a
Veffel, or whether we fee it in
drops, or in the form of a Scum,
or whether it rife in Vapours, or
whether, remaining without motion, it appear in Ice or Snow.

We know alfo, that he fuppo-
feth, that there hath been a great
number of thefe particles very
fmooth and very pliant, mingled
with other bodies, a great part
of

of which had figures so embaras-
sing, that their Aggregate could
form no other but hard Masses.

Lastly, We know, that he supposeth these last particles have been
the matter of many Masses almost
like the Earth; and forasmuch as
theseMasses could not be very so-
lid&very hard,but by an extream
pressing of the Branchy particles which compose them, it is
evident, that the particles of
water which were mixed therewith, were driven out of it, and
that so the surfaces of those great
Masses were to be altogether covered with it.

This being supposed, it is now
to be observed, that, according
to M. *Des Cartes*, the formation
of the Firmament is nothing else
but a perfect disposition and ranging of all the Whirlpools, of
which I have already spoken in

B 2   the

the Subject of Light : Their
number is fo great, and the fpace
they fill fo vaft, that the word
Firmament, according to the tru-
eft interpretation, fignifieth a vaft
extenfion. There is nothing that
deferveth more this name, than
their Aggregate. But as we
ought to mark the time of the
formation of every thing, only
from the moment which giveth it
its perfection ; M. *Des Cartes* having fuppofed, that the Aggregate of all the whirlpools was not
yet well ordered, when the Light
began, nor their motion very
free, doth mark the time of the
formation of the Firmament, then
only, when they were fo well adjufted, that the Ecliptick of the
one anfwering to the Poles of
the other, they began to move
among themfelves with a motion
altogether free, and fo propor-
tioned,

tioned, that not any one received a Let from all thofe,which
encompaffed it.

'Tis at this inftant, that, according to *Des Cartes's* Hypothefis, the Maffes, which were in
the fame *Vortex*, where the Earth
was,began to be feparated from it
by the matter of that *Vortex*,
which infinuated it felf betwixt
them, and which kept them more
or lefs diftant from the Center,
according to the difference of
their grofsnefs or folidity. Now,
as we have noted, that they were
all covered with their Waters,
and that the matter of the *Vortexes* (which, according to this
Doctrine, is the matter of the
Firmament) feparated them from
the Earth, it was true to fay, following the fame Doctrine as well
as that of *Genefis*, that the Waters were fevered from the Wa-

B 3   ters,

ters, by the formation of the Firmament.

Thus M. *Des Cartes*, who seems
always to follow *Moses*, disposeth the Waters so, that they
are some above, and some under
the Firmament. For we know,
that what the Prophet calls in
this place *Under*, is the Earth we
inhabit; and all that is severed
from it by the Celestial matter,
may be said, in respect of us, to
be above the Firmament.

I do not explain this more at
large, nor do I examine, how
well these different Conservato-
ries of Waters, which M. *Des
Cartes* placeth in several parts of
Heaven, do represent those Cataracts, whence the Lord drew
forth, at the time of his wrath,
what served to overwhelm the
Earth.

Neither do I make reflection
upon

170

upon the Changes, which have happened to the Earth by this super-abundance of Waters. This is perhaps the cause of the Clouds, Rains, and the first apparition of that admirable *Phænomenon*, which the Lord made use of to secure *Noah* against the apprehensions of a new Deluge, when he promised him to shut up for ever those Cataracts, which he had opened for his vengeance ; but this would carry us too far.

B 4   The

The THIRD DAY.

THe *Third* Day *Moſes* obſer-
veth, that, the Waters co-
vering the Globe of the Earth,
it was convenient to gather them
together into certain places, to
the end that the other parts
thereof remaining diſcovered,
the Earth might produce Herbs,
Plants and Trees of all kinds.
He ſaith, that the ſame word,
which had operated the wonders
of the precedent days, wrought
that alſo. To which he adds,
that what appeared dry, was
called *Earth*, and the collection
of the Waters, *Sea.*,

**Now it is evident, that if the
Earth**

Earth had remained perfectly
round, the waters could not have
been gathered into places, to
leave others dry. We muſt therefore believe, that the ſame day,
which ſaw the ſeparation of the
Waters from the Earth, ſaw alſo
the formation of the Hills, and
that certain parts of the Earth
being raiſed above others, left
Vallies betwixt them for Beds to
the waters, and Cavities under
their Elevations, to receive a
quantity of water, approaching
to that which ſhould appear no
more. 'Tis thus, that M. *Des
Cartes* explicateth the matter. He
declareth alſo, how the Earth was
enabled to produce herbs, plants
and trees, and how the different
Juices, which run within the bo-
ſom of the Earth inſinuate themſelves into ſeveral Seeds, whoſe
pores are adapted to their figure.

I

I defire you in this place to obferve, that *Mofes* faith not, that
God made any *Soul* for Plants;
he only faith, that the Earth, rendred fertile by the word of the
Lord, did produce them.   But
thofe Philofophers who have alwaies had recourfe to Souls, when
they would explicate the effects
of certain Organical Bodies, of
which they could not difcover
the Springs, have given one to
every Plant.   They have believed, that it was impoffible, to
give an accompt of Vegetation
without it.   But M. *Des Cartes*,
without adding any thing to the
Scripture, where *Mofes* fpeaketh
of Plants, of their Seeds, of
their increafe and fruit without
fpeaking of any Soul, hath believed, there needed none to be
fuppofed to give a reafon of their
Nutrition; and he hath fo clearly

ly shewed, that Vegetation is
performed by the local motion
of the parts which come in afresh,
and by the fitness of their figure
to the pores of that plant, which
they are proper to increase, that
I think I may assure, that there is
none, how little soever accustomed to Ratiocination, but will acknowledge, after he hath examined what he saith on this Subject, that there remains not the
least probability to maintain, that
Plants have Souls.

Yet you know, that there are
yet some who will defend, that
there are *Vegetative* Souls. But
what, I pray, can authorize
them? Not Reason surely. *That*
tells us all, that things ought not
to be multiplied without necessity; and since we do manifestly
fee, that Figure and Motion may
be the entire cause of Vegetation,

we

175

we ought not to no purpose have recourse to Souls. Nor can it be the Authority either of Man, or of the H. Scripture; for that of Man cannot be considerable against the evidence of natural Notions, and against the Experiments by which this Errour is convinced. As to that of Sacred Writ, it is manifest, that that is not on their side, and nothing appears there that may come near to what they would attribute to Plants, *viz.* a Vegetative Soul.

The

The Fourth Day.

THe *Fourth* Word did form two great Luminaries in the Firmament, to divide perfectly the Day from the Night, and to mark the difference of Dayes, Seasons and Years. The same Word formed also the Stars, according to the History of *Moses*.

M. *Des Cartes* explaining this as a Naturalist, saith, that the several *Vortexes*, which had been formed of all the Celestial matter, having been adapted to one another, as was most convenient for the continuation of their motions, there flowed so much of the most subtil matter towards the

the Center of each of them, by
the preſſure of the *Globules*, which
tended to recede from it, that at
length each of the Whirlpools
came to have in his middle ſo
great a quantity of this matter,
that it was able to propel the globules to the extremities of the
Whirlpool, and by this action to
form ſuch Rays, as thoſe are,
whoſe force makes us ſee the ſhining Sun.

He adds, that this ſubtil matter, gathered at the Center of
each *Vortex*, may have force e-
nough to thruſt the Globules of
the Neighbouring *Vortexes*, and
to make there its action ſenſible.
So that, according to this Author, the ſhining collection of
ſubtil matter, which was made
in the Center of this *Vortex*
wherein was the Earth, was, in
reſpect of it, the greateſt Luminary,

nary, that is, the *Sun*: Thofe
that were made in the other *Vortexes*, were *Stars* ; and *that* of all
the great Maffes,which was found
neareft,and moft difpofed to propel towards it the Light of the
Sun,was the leffer Luminary,that
is, the *Moon*. I fhall fay no more
of it; and 'tis fo well known,
that the difference of Dayes,
Nights and Seafons comes from
the different fituation, wherein
the Earth, the Sun & other Stars
are found, that I fhould be tedious to repeat here what M. *Des
Cartes* hath written on this Subject.

The

The Fifth & Sixth Day.

THe *Fifth* Day God said;
*Let the Waters produce the
Moving Creature that hath a living Soul, and Fowl that fly above
the Earth.* And the *Sixth* Day
he said, *Let the Earth bring forth
the Living Creature after its kind,
Cattel, and creeping things, and
Beasts of the Earth.* I do not
add the rest; for it is enough to
say, that God would have it so,
to let men know, that it was
so.

This Place teaching us, that
if it may be said, that Fish and the
other Brute Animals have Souls,
these

180

thefe Souls are produced by the
Waters and the Earth ; M. *Des
Cartes* had reafon to believe, that
what is here called Soul, is nothing elfe but little Bodies fo adjufted to the Organs of Fifhes
and other Brutes, that they make
them live, move and grow:

He hath admirably explained
upon this Subject the Circulation
of the Bloud ; the manner *how*
it is heated in the Heart ; *how* it
runs into the Arteries, whofe different pores let out the particles,
which their figure maketh fit for
the nourifhment of the Members;
and *how* the fineft parts of all extricate themfelves from the reft,
to go to the Brain, whence they
are diftributed into Mufcles,
where they ferve for the motion
of the whole Body.

He doth give fuch an accurate
accompt of all thefe things only

C   by

by the figure and the motion of
the little Bodies, and the difpofition of the Organs, that there
can remain no doubt of them.
And that it may not feem a wonder, what he faith of the heat of
the Bloud, which he maketh the
chief Spring of all thofe Functions, commonly called Vital and
Animal, he proves, that they muft
neceffarily be performed by Bodies, without the need of any
Soul ; adding to his Reafons the
example of certain Liquors,
which are cold to the touch when
they are afunder, but grow prefently hot, even to a degree of e-
bullition, when they are blended
together. As this effervefcence
happens to Liquors, which are
not fo much as fufpected to
have Souls, M. *Des Cartes* hath,
me thinks, advanced nothing but
what is rational, when he faith,
     That

That the heat of the Bloud, join-
ed to the difpofition and the de-
pendance of the Organs, is able
without a Soul to caufe the nutrition and motion of Brutes.

Me thinks alfo, that he had
reafon, fince, what the *Vulgar
Tranflation* calls a *Living Soul*, was
produced by the Waters and the
Earth, to believe, that this kind
of Souls were only Bodies. And
indeed there are fo many places,
whereby we may know, that this
was the meaning of *Mofes*, that
'tis a wonder to me to find men
ftill doubting thereof.

I fhould tire you to recite them
all to you; let me only defire
you to reflect a little on *Lev.* 17.
11. where you will plainly find
what it is that enlivens Flefh and
Beafts; *The Soul of all Flefh is in
the Bloud.* The fame faith M. *Des
Cartes.* But *Deut.* 12. 23. *Mofes*

C 2   expref-

expresseth himself yet more
clearly, to make us understand,
that Beasts have no other Souls
than the Bloud : *Only be sure that
thou eat not the Bloud : for the
Bloud is the Soul.* And that it
might be yet more understood,
he adds ; *And therefore thou maist
not eat the Soul , but shalt pour it
upon the Earth as water.* Is there
not then all the reason in the
world, that those Souls, which
the earth produceth, which may
be eaten, and poured out upon
the earth as water , should be
counted among Bodies ?

I grant indeed, that the bloud,
when it is heated, is exhaled in
very subtil parts, and that these
fine parts are those , which do
nourish and move. But how
subtil soever they be , they are
Bodies, and they have nothing
more of spiritual in them, than
flame,

flame, compofed of parts yet more
fubtil, which yet never any man
was fo unadvifed as to call fpiri-
tual.

I wonder for my part, that
thofe who have given Souls to all
that is nourifh'd, have given none
to a Flame, which converts into it
all the bodies it lays hold on. And
(what is more) I wonder, how
men could come to attribute to
Souls the caufe of Nutrition and
Motion, whereas we fee nothing
but Body that is capable to be
moved, and that Nutrition is nothing elfe but an addition of Bodies to Bodies, But without infifting fo much upon Ratiocination, is
it not vifible, that *Mofes* (who certainly ought to be believed) ac-
knowledges no other thing for
the caufe of the motion and nutrition of Beafts, but the bloud?
I think not, that any man, who

C 3   con-

confiders it, will contend about
it any longer.

But that you may the better
know the force of all thefe paf-
fages, which hitherto I have only taken according to the *Vulgar
Tranflation*, and which, according to this verfion, leave no difficulty, although the word *Soul*
have been thefe employed; I
fhall now make ufe of a means,
which wil prevail upon your fpirit , and better perfwade you
than any other.

You know more than one Language; and among others you
know the *Hebrew*, which I underftand not. I fhall tell you then,
that a while ago, reflecting on
that place of Scripture, where is
defcribed the work of the Fifth,
and that of the Sixth Day, there
appeared to me fo great a difference betwixt the manner , in
which

186

which the formation of Brutes, and that of Man was made, that I believed, what word foever was ufed in the *Vulgar*, there muft be ufed very differing Expreffions in the *Hebrew*.

I faw, that the *Vulgar* faid, that the Beafts have a *Living Soul*, and that the fame Tranflation ufed the fame word to fignifie the *Life* of Man: But I found withal, that befides that living Soul, which the *Vulgar* gives to Man, as it doth to Brutes, 'tis added, that Man was made to the Image of his Maker, whom I knew to be a pure Spirit. Whence I concluded, that fince this Refemblance could not be drawn from the Body, the Creator having none, it muft needs be taken from fomething of a fuperiour order, and, in a word, from the Spirit. To this I added, what the *Vulgar* expreffeth

C 4

preſſeth, ſpeaking of Man in the
Second *Chap.* of *Gen.* Where I
ſaw , that the Lord , who had
made him a living Creature, as
the Beaſts , had breathed into
him ſomething which Beaſts had
not , and which , me thought ,
ſhould be in him the Principle of
a Life altogether different from
theirs, and the cauſe of that ad-
vantageous reſemblance , which
he was to have with his Maker.

All theſe things did already
ſway much with me for the advantage of Man ; but believing
that I might yet better diſcover
the ſenſe of thoſe places, by getting the Interpretation of the *Hebrew*, I conſulted Monſieur *de
Compiegne*, who is known to be
the ableſt we have in this Language. I prayed him to give me
the Verſion of the firſt and ſecond Chapter of *Geneſis* ; and in
this

this Verfion I found the full
proof of what I always thought,
and of what M. *Des Cartes* had
written on this Subject. For I
faw, that in the place, which
fpeaks of the Production of
Fifhes and other Brutes, where
the *Vulgar* faith, Let the Waters
and the Earth bring forth *Living
Souls*, my Interpreter faid, Let
the Earth and the Water produce
Living *Individuals* : which car-
rieth with it a very good fenfe,
and expreffeth the thing in a far
more conceivable manner : For,
it is very intelligible, that the
Earth and Waters have produced
living *Individuals*, that is, that they
have been fo fitted and difpofed
by the Almighty hand of the
Lord, as to form Organical Bodies, which being fit for Nutrition and Motion (in which confifts all the *Life* of Bodies) were
to

189

to be called *Living*; but forasmuch as they could not be divided without being quite destroyed, were to be called *Individuals*.

Secondly, I see in the place which speaks of the formation of *Man*, that not only he was formed out of the Earth by the hands of the Lord, and that thereby he was become a *Living Individual*, as Beasts are; but above that, I see, that besides this Individual or Body Organick, which maketh him feed & move like Beasts, he hath received another thing, which my Interpreter calls *Mens*, and which I call Spirit, or Thought.

So that, as there is nothing spoken of a Soul for Plants in the Vulgar (as I have already observed) so there is neither in the *Hebrew* for Brutes. Neither is it said,

said, that Brutes have *Senfe*, (which I alfo defire you to note) but this only is faid, that they have Life and Motion. And becaufe this Life and this Motion do depend upon the difpofition and correfpondence of many Organs, the *Divifion* of which would hinder the effect; *Mofes*, to fignifie this Aggregate by one word, ufeth that of נפש, which fignifieth *Individual*.

But that, which we ought to confider above all, is, what the fame facred Writer fo well declareth; *That* Man hath a Body organized as Brutes have, and *that* this Body liveth by the fame Principles which give life to Brutes; *that* having faid, that the *Individuum* of every Beaft was produced by the Waters and the Earth, he faith, that that of Man was alfo produced of the Earth.

Earth. And to make us understand, that this dust of the earth,
which before was divisible without danger, was so disposed that
it became an *Individual*, as every one of the other living bodies;
he expresseth himself by the same
word he used speaking of Beasts;
and at the same time adds, that
the Lord inspired into this living
Individual, of which he would
make a man, that which he expresseth by the word נשמה, that
is, a *Spirit*, or *Thought*.

This seems to me so strong,
that I think there can remain no
more scruple about this point,
viz. what we are to believe hence-
forth of Brutes and of Man. *Moses* hath given us clearly to understand, that Brutes live and move,
because the Bloud and the contrivance of their Organs maketh
of each of them an Individual
Body

Body, which remains fit for thofe
two effects, as long as that contrivance lafts: And why fhould
we attribute any other thing to
them but this individual body,
by which an accompt can be given of their Life and Motion?

But then, *Mofes* faith not, that
they have *Senfe*. Why fhould we
devife, that they have any? Or,
at leaft, what danger is there to
affert, that they have none?

Laftly, this Man, infpired by
God, teacheth us, that the Brutes
have nothing but what a Body
may have, and that we have a
body as they. But he adds, that
we have befides a *Spirit* ; or, if
you will, a Soul, which we know
is alone capable of having fenfe,
of judging, of willing, and of all
the other wayes of *thinking*. Why
then fhould we not affert, that
the brute Animals have nothing
but

but Body, and that they have no
ſentiment ? And why ſhould we
not affirm, that beſides a body,
like unto that which they have,
(which maketh us not reſemble
our Maker)we have a Soul,which
giveth us that admirable advantage to reſemble him as much as
a Creature is capable to do ?

If after all this you ſhall ſtill
tell me,that the opinion of M.*Des
Cartes* is dangerous, in that it
maketh Brutes live and move
without a ſoul; I ſhall anſwer
you, that then the Hiſtory of
Moſes is dangerous, foraſmuch as
it teacheth us the ſame thing.

But if, after you have ſeen,
how well *Moſes* doth ſeparate
that in Man, which maketh him
live and move, from that which
maketh him *think*, you ſhall examine, how the Creed of S. *Atha-
naſius,* which we read every day
as

as the Symbol of our Faith, defi-
neth *Man*, you'l fee, that he faith,
that the Flefh, and the Rational
Soul make all what he is : To
which he adds, that, as thefe two
fubftances, how different foever
they be, conftitute but one man ;
fo God and Man make but one
and the fame Chrift. But as in
our Lord *Jefus Chrift* it is not allowed , whatever the Union of
his two Natures be, to confound
them fo, as to attribute to the one
what comes from the other ; fo
there is alwayes great danger to
confound in Man the two Sub-
ftances which do compofe him,
and the Functions which depend
from each of them.

Thofe that give to the Body
fentiment or other perceptions,
which cannot belong but to the
Soul, are fubject to believe, that
Man, as a Beaft , hath nothing
but

but Body. On the other hand,
thofe who think, that the Soul is
that which caufeth Nutrition and
Motion in Man, are liable to believe, that the Beafts, which feed
and move, have a Soul as Man
hath ; and when there is no other
difference betwixt Souls than
that of *more* or *lefs*, there is an
Axiom, which faying, *That more
or lefs changeth not the Effence*, maketh, that Men will foon accuftom
themfelves to believe, that if all
perifheth in Beafts by death, there
remains alfo nothing in Man, when
he hath loft his Life.

As for me, I doubt not at all,
but what hath been faid of Vegetative and Senfitive Souls, which
are attributed to Plants and to
Beafts, hath made impious men
believe, that thofe which are given to men, may be of the fame
nature.

If

If my Difcourfe were not too prolix already, I could explain to you the moft wonderful operations of Brutes by the fole Conftruction of their Organs, as all the operations of a Watch are made out to you by the contrivance of its parts; and fhew you, that there is no difference betwixt Artificial and Natural Engines, but in this, that the Author of Nature is a far more excellent Artift than Men are, and that he hath known to apply fuch parts to one another, as are much fubtiler and much nimbler than thofe are of which we commonly compofe our Machines. I could alfe demonftrate to you, that there is nothing known to us in Brutes, even in the *Ape* it felf, which may not be explicated from Bodies; and that in Man there are *Thoughts,* which all the

D diver-

diverſities imaginable in Figures
and Motions cannot give an accompt of. But I ſhould exceed
the Bounds I have preſcribed to
my ſelf, and it ſufficeth me to
have ſhewed you, that M. *Des
Cartes* hath alwayes followed
Moſes, to make you aver, that
his Philoſophy contains nothing
dangerous.

Mean time I ſhall acknowledge,
that the formation of the World
according to M. *Des Cartes*, ſeems
to have ſomething different from
that of *Moſes*. But when you
ſhall have conſidered the Deſign
of the Prophet, and alſo that of
the Philoſopher, you will confeſs
that this difference ought not to
make us ſay, that they have re-
ceded from one another.

Moſes hath delivered the thing
as 'twas done. He ſaith, that God
created the Earth, the Waters,
the

the Celestial Parts, then the Light,
and the rest; so that, when the
Sun was created, the Earth was
already inriched with Fruits, and
adorned with Flowers. Whereas
M. *Des Cartes* maketh the Sun
the Cause, not only of the Fruits,
and Flowers, but also of the
gathering together of many inward parts of the Earth. The
same also maketh the Earth to
have been formed a long time
after the Sun, although the Scripture noteth, that it was created
before.

But here we are to take notice
of 2 things: The *one* is, that M. *Des
Cartes* hath said himself, that his
Hypothesis was false in this, that
he supposeth that the formation
of each Being is made successivly;
assuring, that this way not being
so proper for God, we are to believe, that his Omnipotency hath

D 2   put

put every thing in the most perfect condition it could be in, from the first moment of its production.

The *other* is, that M. *Des Cartes* was, like a Philosopher, to explicate only the reason, why things are conserved as they are, and the different effects we now admire in Nature. Now, as 'tis certain, that things are naturally conserved by the same means which hath produced them; so it was necessary for to find, whether the Laws, which he supposeth Nature follows to conserve her self, are true, that he should examine, whether the same Laws could have disposed it as now it is : And finding, that according to the History of *Moses* it self, although the Sun was formed after the Earth, it is yet by the Sun, that God conserveth the Earth as now

now it is, the heat thereof being cause of all the Productions and Changes therein ; M. *Des Cartes* was to shew, that this same Sun could have put it into that state we now find it in, if the great Creator had not put it there in an instant by his Omnipotent power.

'Tis true indeed, that the manner, in which M. *Des Cartes* describeth , that the Sun hath disposed the Earth , is successive, which he acknowledgeth (as I have already noted) to be not so sutable to God in producing things : But however, as that which God doth in conserving the World , is successive , and must be so, that every thing may have a certain duration ; it was proper for our Philosopher to examine, whether the Principles which he laid down to give an

D 3   accompt

accompt of the duration of all
Natural Beings, could have produced them by fucceffion of
time; which he hath done with
an exactness, which feems to me
incomparable. And fo M. *Des
Cartes* hath therein done nothing,
contrary to the Defign of *Mofes*.

Mofes knew, that 'tis by the
Sun that God conferveth the
Earth and the Natural Beings,
thofe at leaft which are neareft
unto us; but left it fhould be
thought, that that Luminary was
the caufe of all, he would have
us know, that *Light*, which depends moft of all from the Sun,
was made before the Sun. And
this was neceffary to give notice
of to thofe who were to know
thefe Wonders, that God hath
wrought them all by his fole will;
and if he conferveth them now
with

with a kind of mutual Dependency, yet they do not owe their Being nor their Confervation to one another, but to God alone.

M. *Des Cartes* on his part, being to explain that correfpondence, which God hath put between the things of Nature, and being to give an accompt by the Sun of all that is done in that part of the World which is moft known to men, could not better declare to us, how well the Sun is fitted and difpofed by the Firft Power to maintain the natural ftate of all we fee, than by fhewing, that, following this fame difpofition, the Sun could have in progrefs of time put our World into the condition 'tis in, if it had not been more proper to form all the Creatures in an Order altogether contrary to that, which was required by the de-

D 4 pendance

pendance that now is between them, and to produce each Being in a way, which might fhew, that as the Author of the World had need of nothing to make all things, fo he needed no time to bring forth any of the things we admire.

Laftly, If you confider, that that Wifdom, which put the firft Man into his moft perfect ftate from the firft moment of his Pro-duction, did fubject his Confer-vation to the fame Laws, from which he hath made to depend the formation of thofe that are born of him, and that, for the right knowledge of the Nature of Man, it would be much more proper to examine the different Changes, which happen in the Seed from the time of Concep-tion, unto the Birth of thofe that are generated, than to examine

the

the miraculous formation of him,
whom Omnipotency finifh'd in
beginning him; you will doubt-
lefs find, that for the well knowing, whether what is taught of
the Laws, which conferve the order of Nature, be true, there is
no better way, than to confider,
whether thofe Laws could have
produced the fame.

I will not examine here, whether what is commonly believed
of the ftability of the Earth, is
better explicated by the Hypothefis of M. *D s Cartes*, than by
thofe which have preceded him.

Neither fhall I examine, whether it be more true than o-
thers; himfelf hath faid (as I
have already noted) that it may
be falfe. And certainly among
an Infinity of ways, which God
may ufe to make one and the fame
thing, it is difficult to affure,
                           which

which that is he hath taken actually. But me thinks , that Men
have reafon to be content, when
they have found one of them,
which can give an accompt of all
the *Phænomena* , and is not contrary to what the H. Scripture
and the Church propofe to us.
M. *Des Cartes* hath been fo fhy to
advance any thing not conform
to what *they* declare to us, that
he hath exprefly fubmitted to the
one, what he feems to have wholly taken out of the other.

Thus whofoever fhall read his
Writings with the fame Spirit,
wherein he wrote them, will not
be in any danger of being deceived, and will be alwayes ready
to acknowledge his Errors , as
foon as thofe that are to direct his
Belief fhall make him underftand
them. As for me, I am perfwa-
ded, that if we fhould condemn
what

what M. *Des Cartes* hath written touching the manner in which the feveral Afpects of the Sun & the Earth are made, and that upon judging, it would not be a fufficient ftability for the Earth, to remain always at reft in the midft of all the Celeftial matter, which is found between the Body of the Moon and it, we fhould come to determine, that the Circle which M. *Des Cartes* makes all that matter run through in 1. year about the Sun, is contrary to what we ought to believe of the reft of the Earth; his greateft Followers, imitating his fubmiffion, would fubmit themfelves firft of all. For in fhort, as they know by evident Demonftrations, not only that 'tis God that is the Caufe of the motion in the leaft portion of the Matter, but alfo that it is his Omnipotent hand which directs

and

ordereth it throughout; it would
be much more eafie for them than
others, to conceieve, that the
fame Hand can direct the Motions
of the Sun, and of all the Celeftial Matter about the Earth, fo
as it fhould not receive the leaft
fhaking from it.

For the reft, I think I cannot
repeat too often, that M. *Des
Cartes* hath not pretended, that
his Hypothefis was true in all, and
hath even acknowledged, that it
was not fo in certain things. But
once more, I efteem, he had reafon to think, that it was allowa-
ble for Men to make fuppofitions,
and that they were all receivable,
fo they did fatisfie all the Appea-
rances, and were not contrary
to Religion.

You'l find in fome of his Letters, that he took much pains,
when he was about to advance
certain

certain Propofitions, to know, whether they had been condemned. It is by the Motives of this difcreet apprehenfion, that he dedicated his Meditations to the Doctors of the *Sorbon*. And in fhort, it appears in his whole Conduct, that he would not for all the knowledge and Honour of the World, run the hazard of an *Anathema*. I muft tell you alfo, that I think I know fome of the beft Wits, which are much addicted to his Tenets; and I know not one of them, that would not abandon them, if they had been condemned. I doubt, whether the fame would be done by thofe that follow *Ariftotle*, if his Opinions fhould be condemned anew : I fay, *anew*, becaufe you know, that they have been fo by the Laws, and even by a Council: And yet, although nothing

nothing have been changed since
in the Canons about it, many
think they may follow him notwithstanding. My chief Design
is not to blame *Aristotle*; I intend
only to justifie M. *Des Cartes*,
and I think I have done it sufficiently, I am,

Reverend Father,

At *Paris,*
Nov.6. 1669. Your Humble and

Obedient Servant,

Des FOURNEILLIS.

THE